AF328486

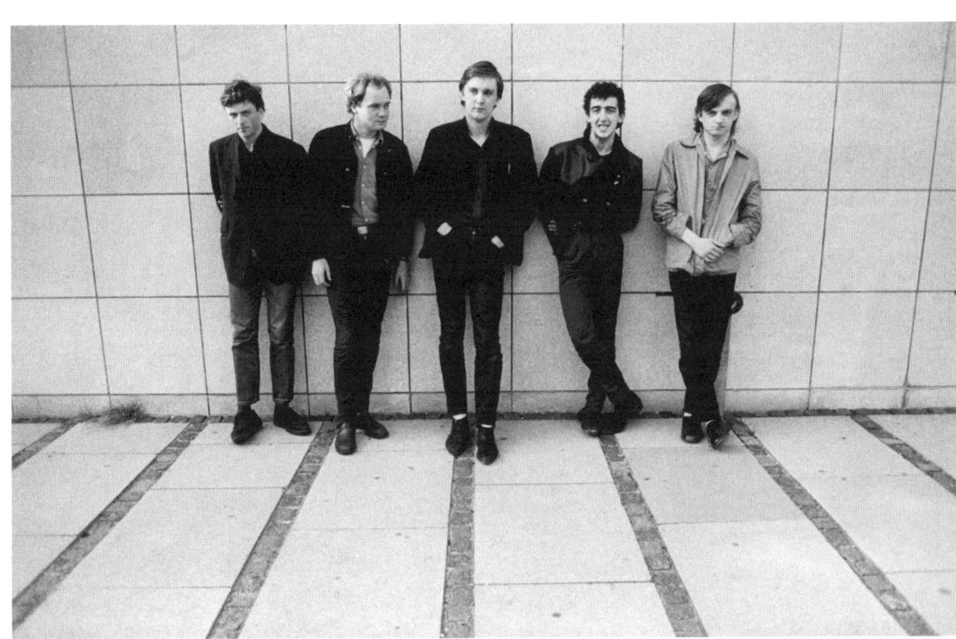

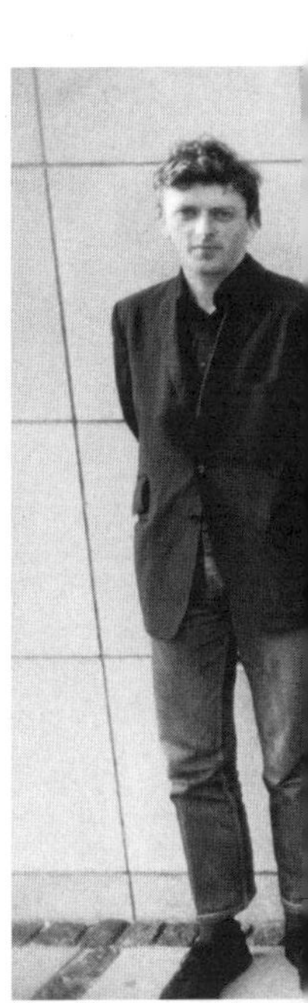

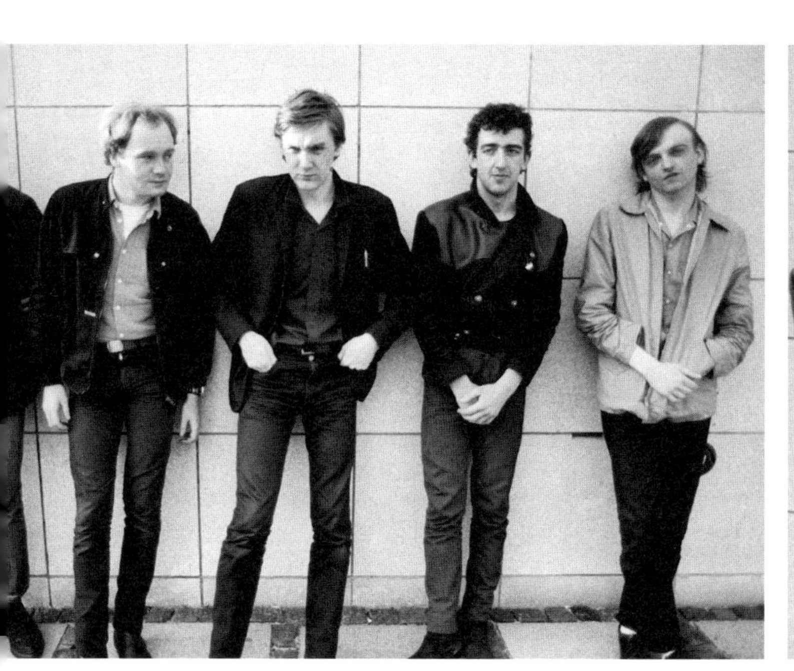
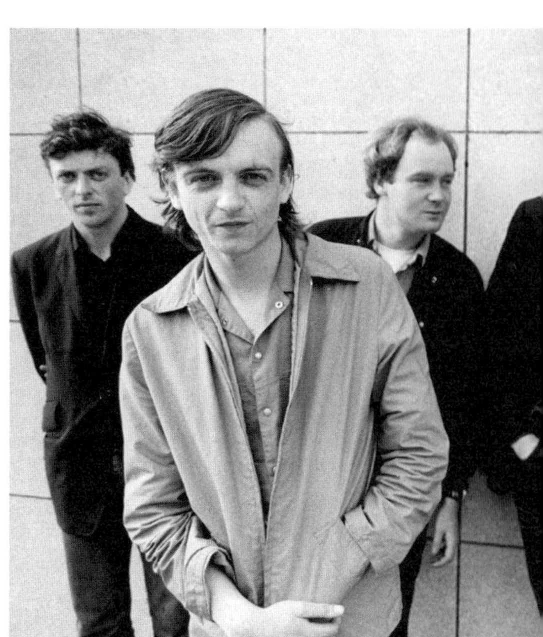

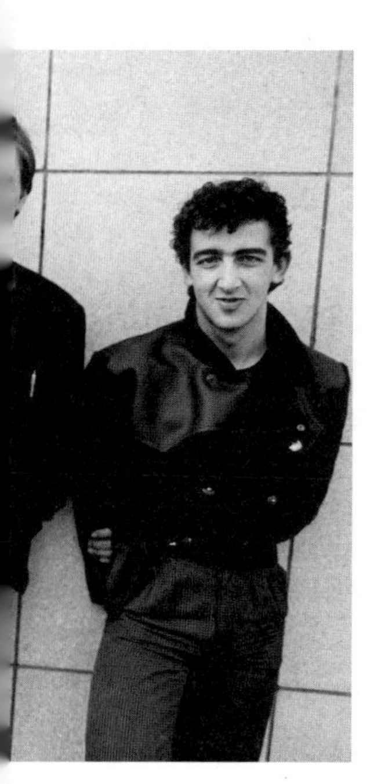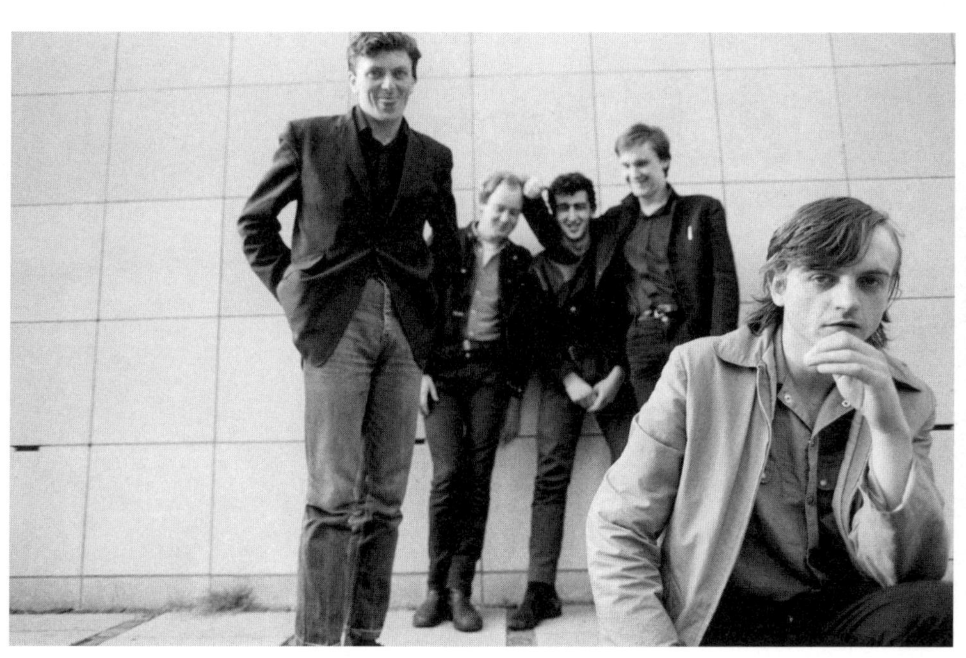

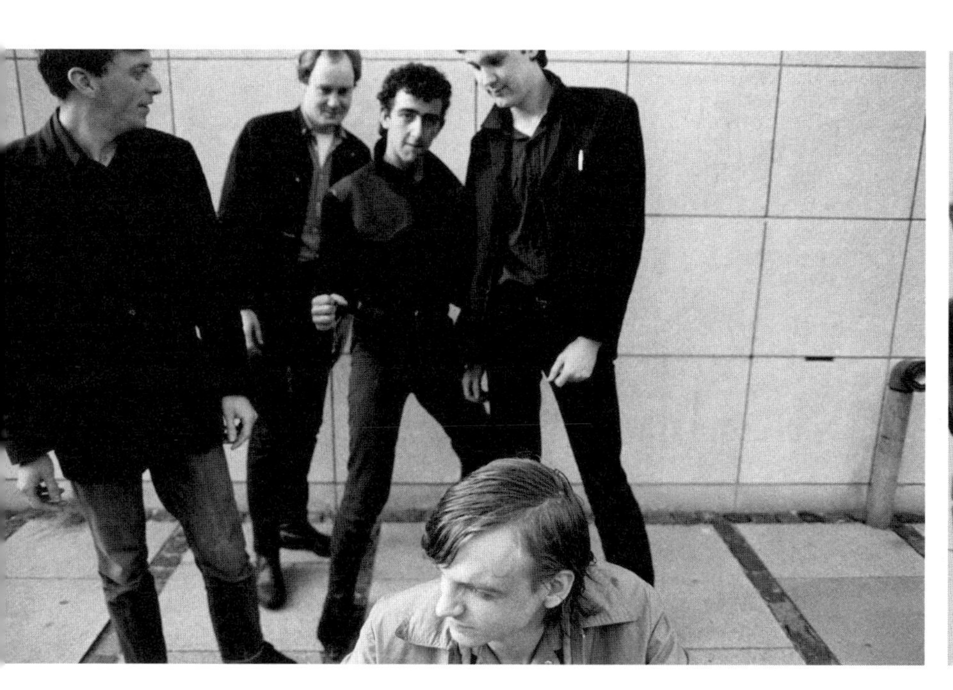
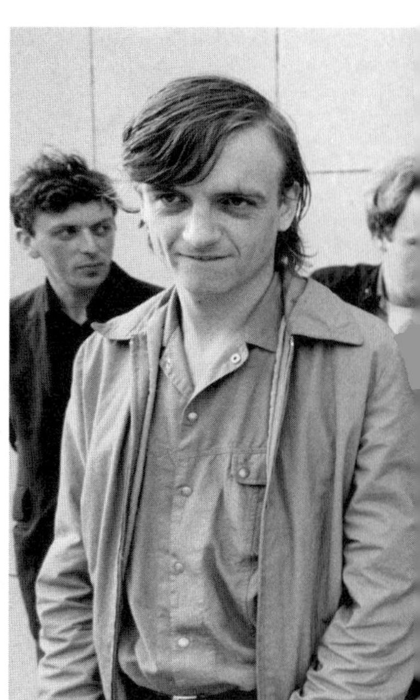

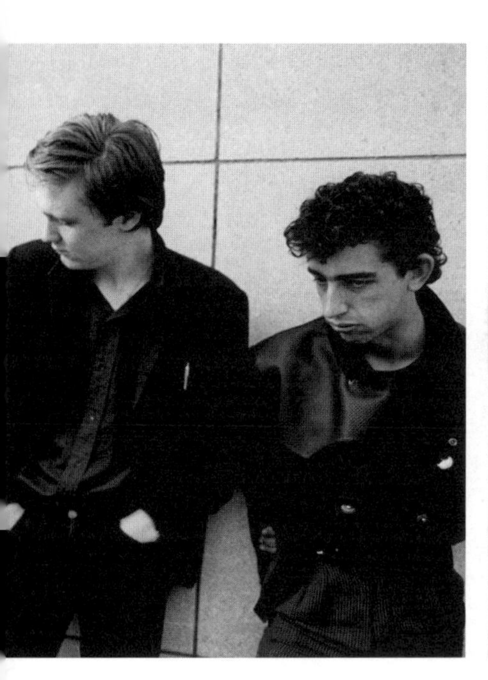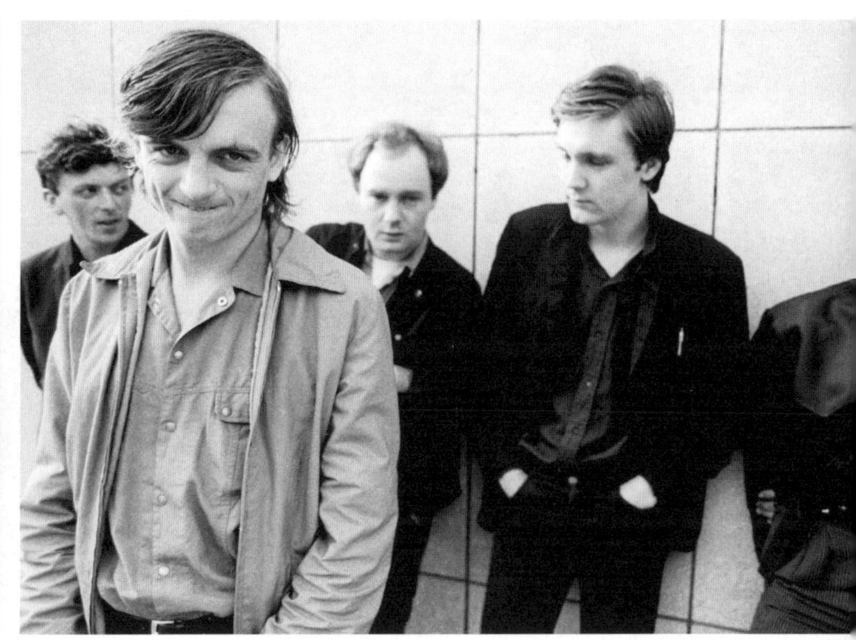

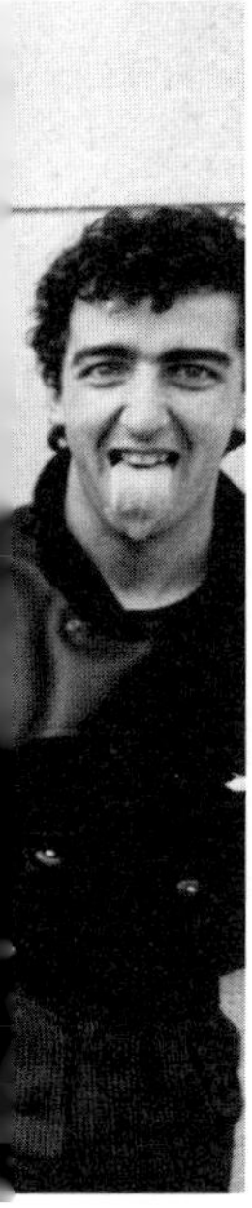

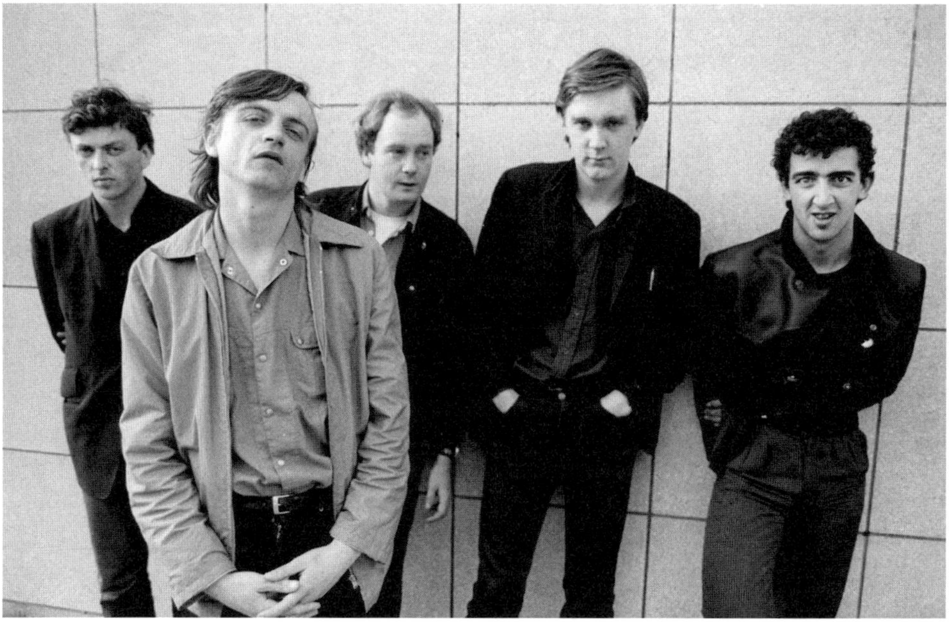

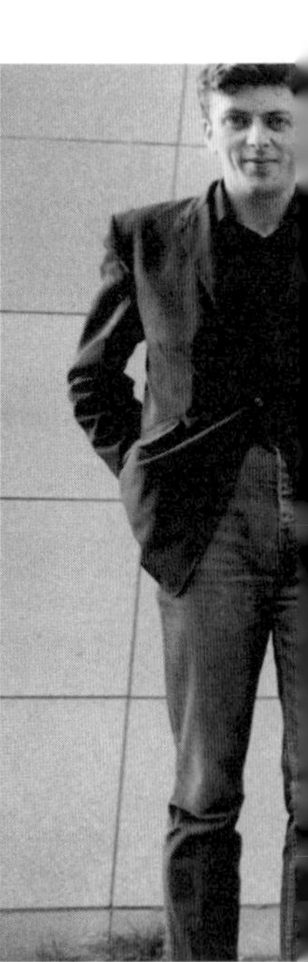

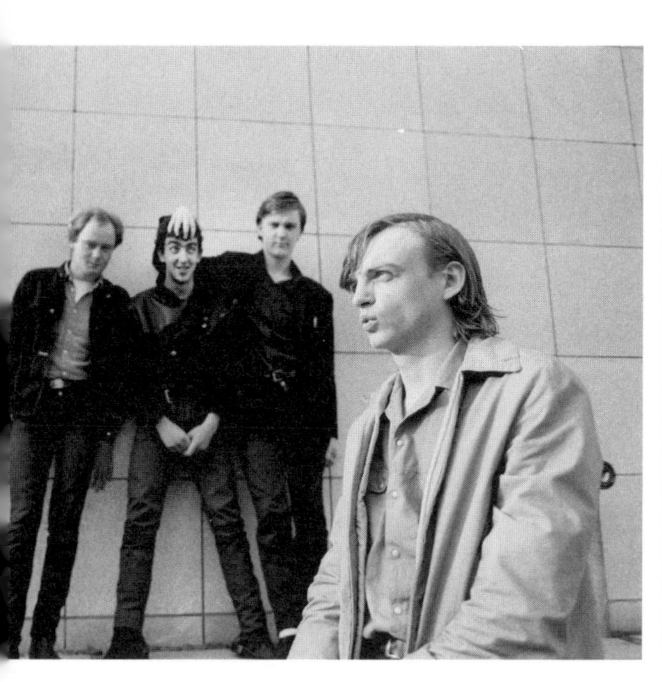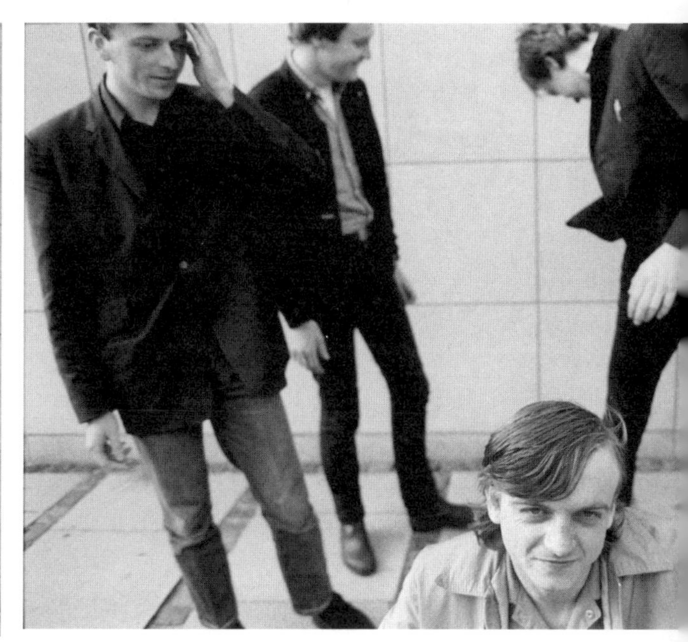

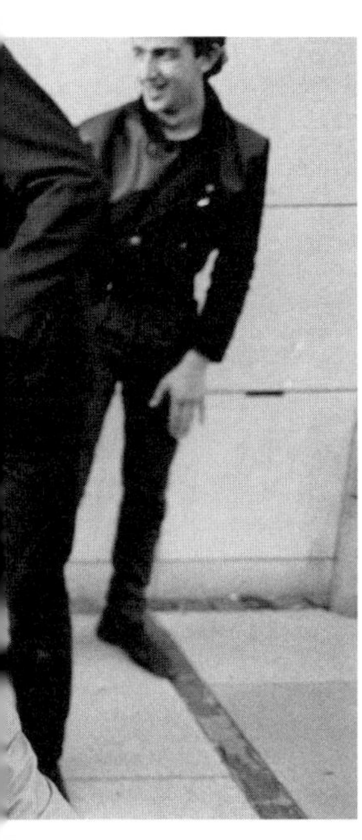

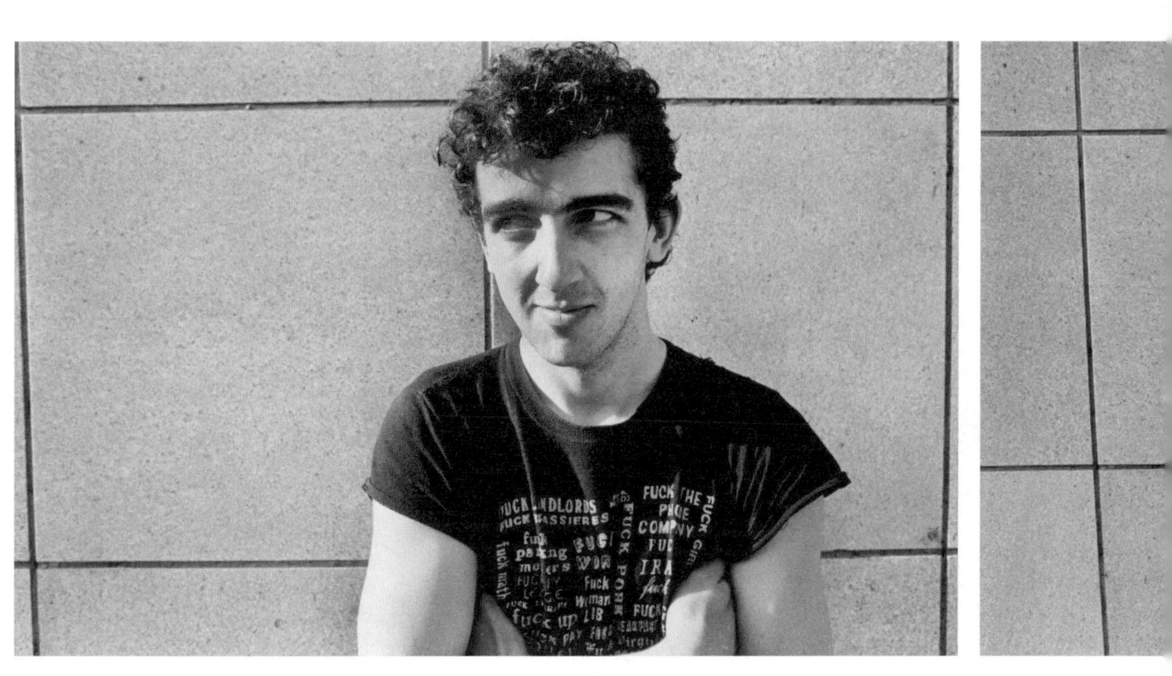

FUCK LANDLORDS
FUCK BASSIERES
FUCK THE
PHOE
COMPNY
fuck
parking
meters
FUCK WOR
FUCK PORK
FUC
IRA
fuck math
Fuck
Woman
LIB
fuck up
FUCK

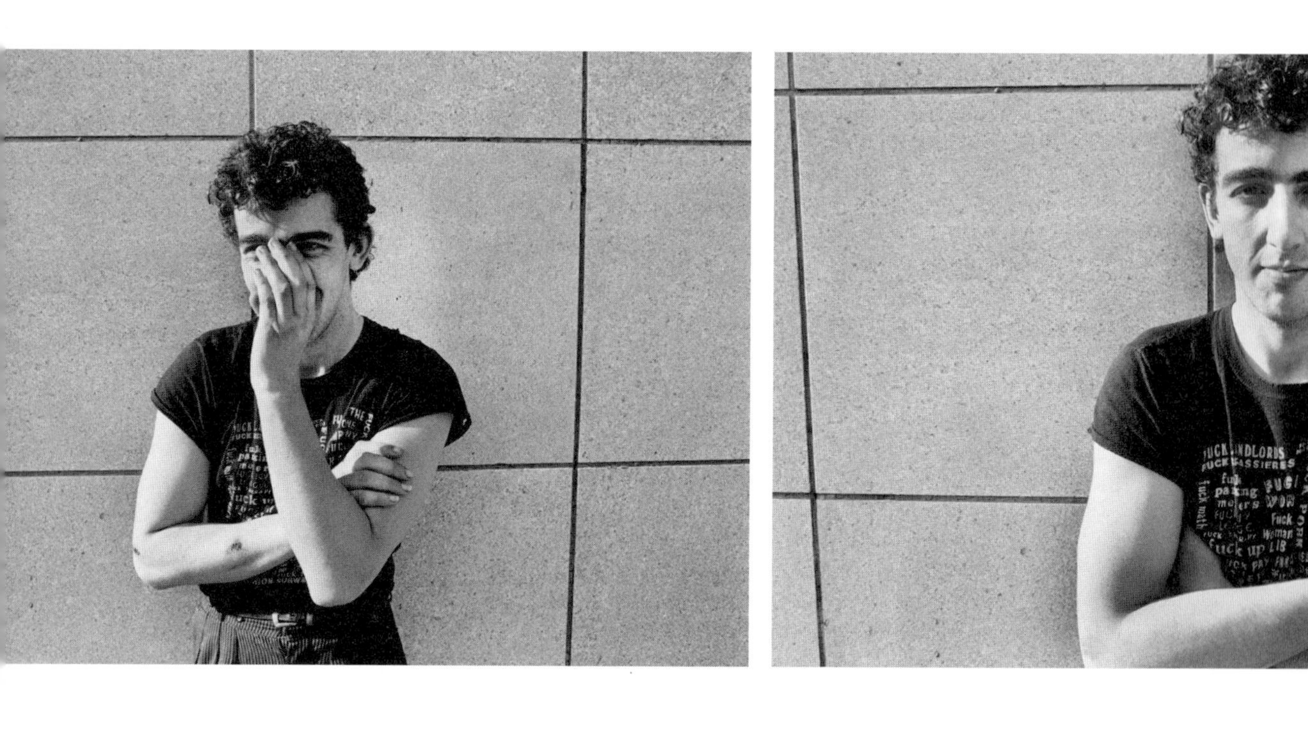

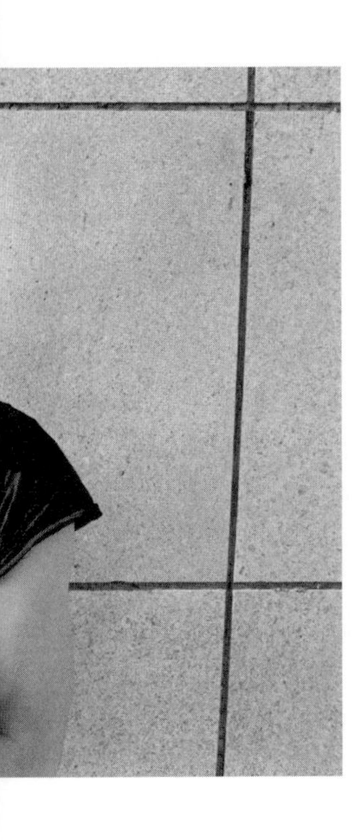

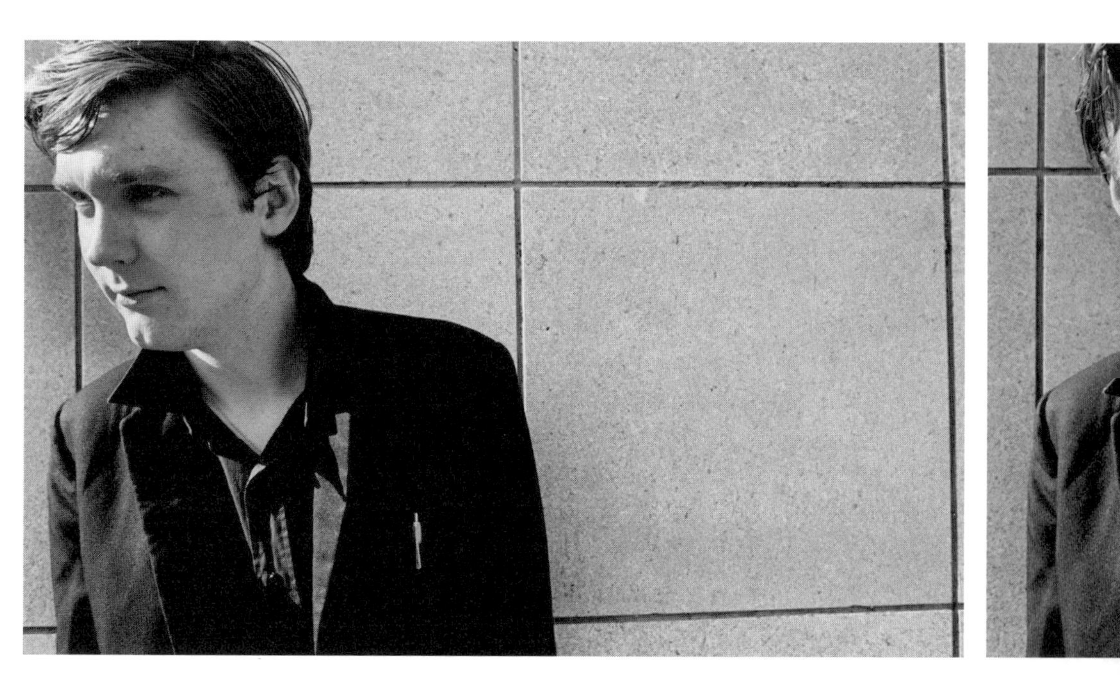

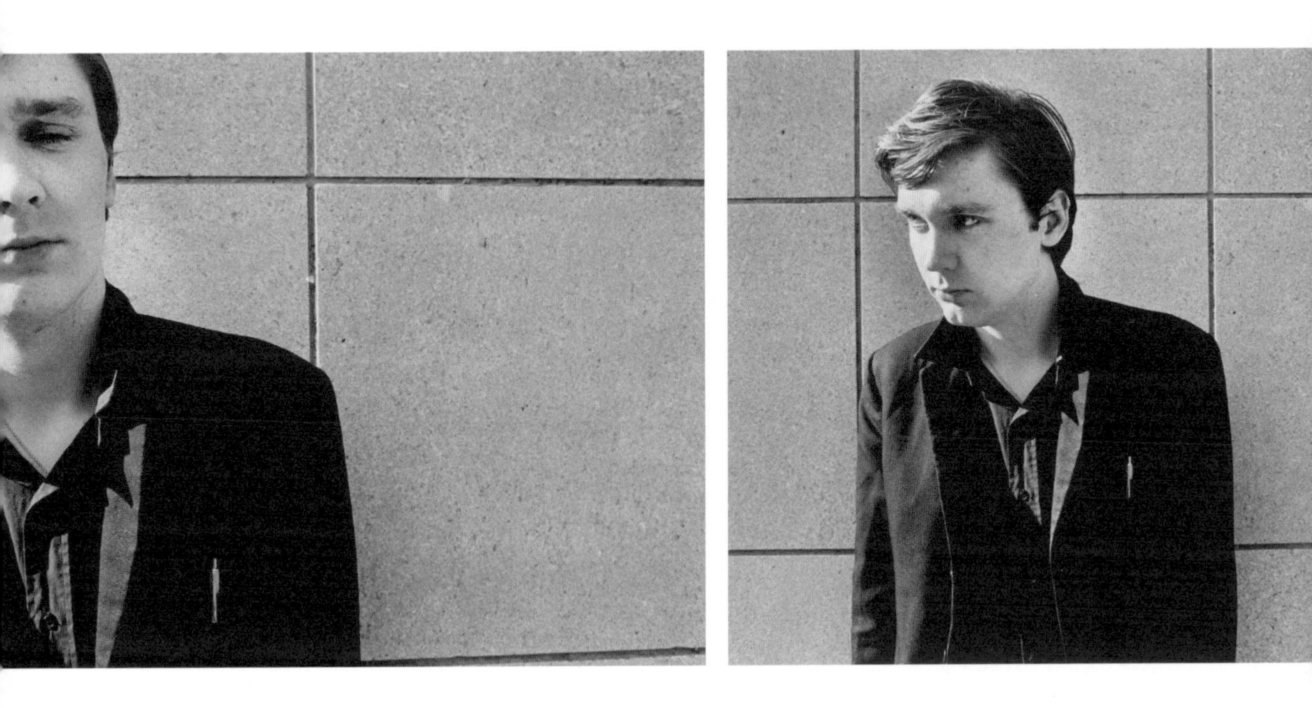

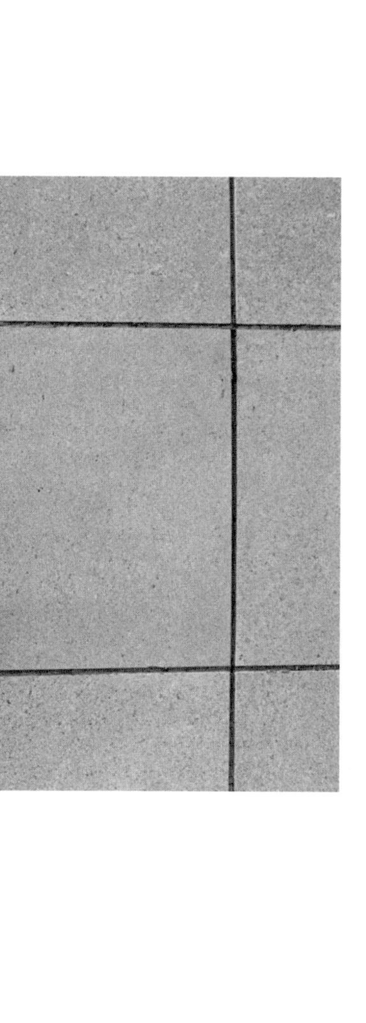

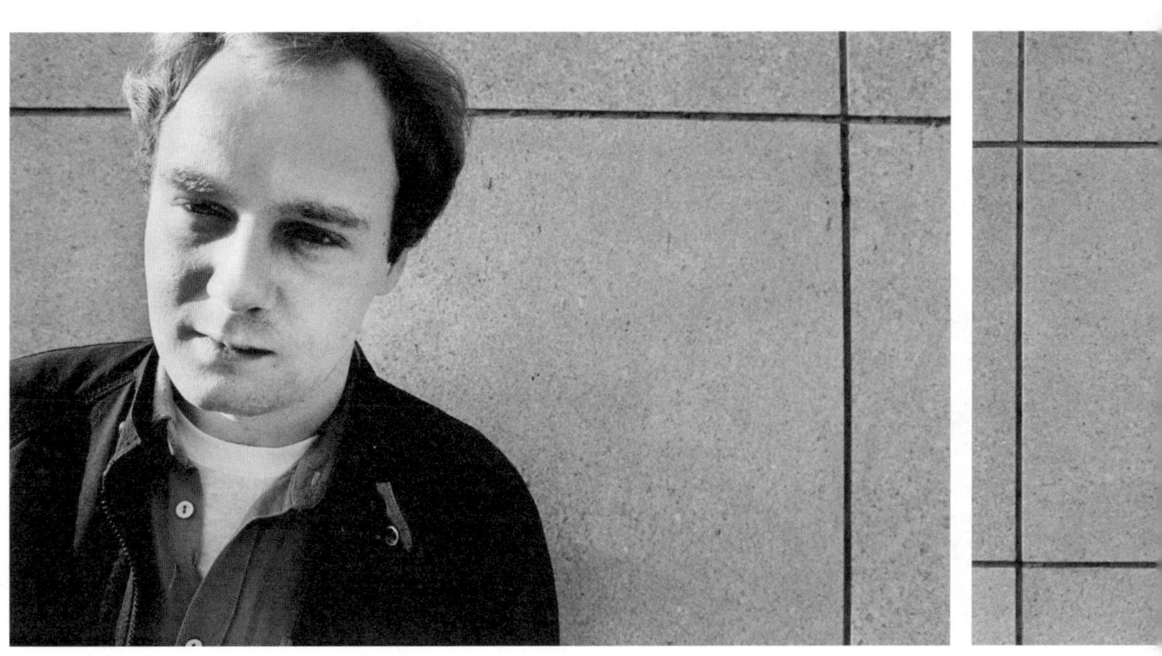

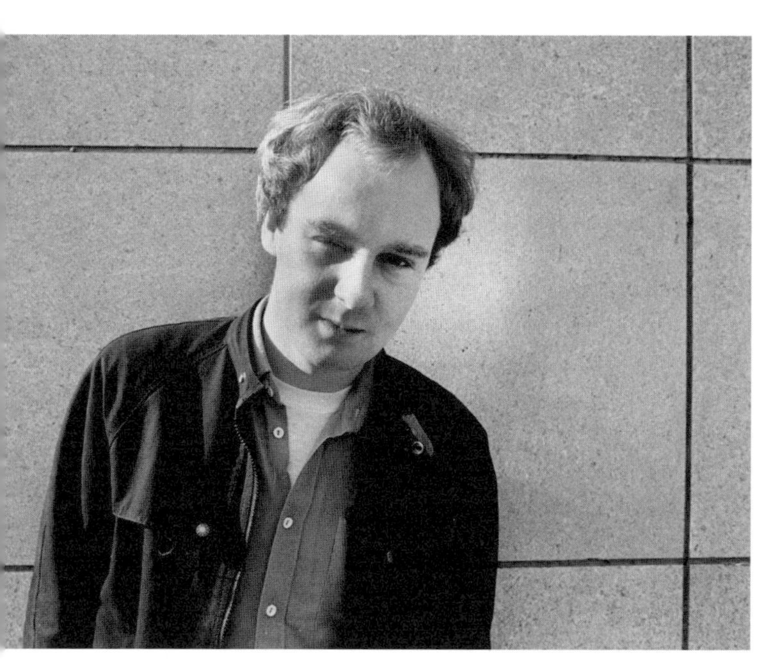

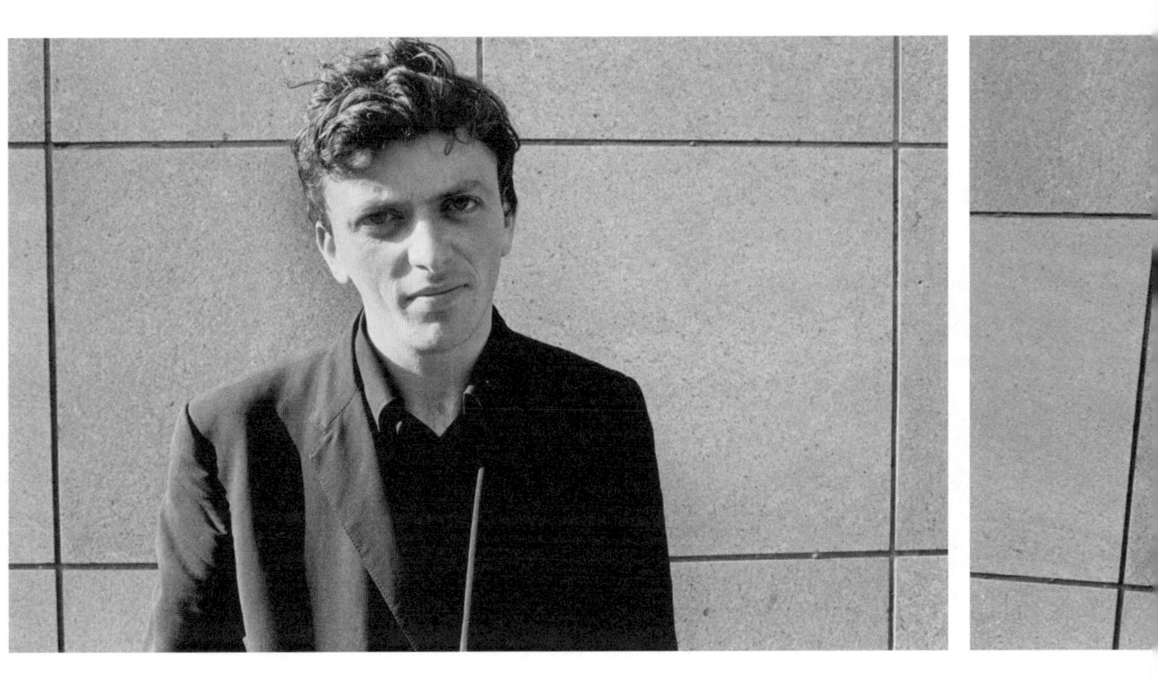

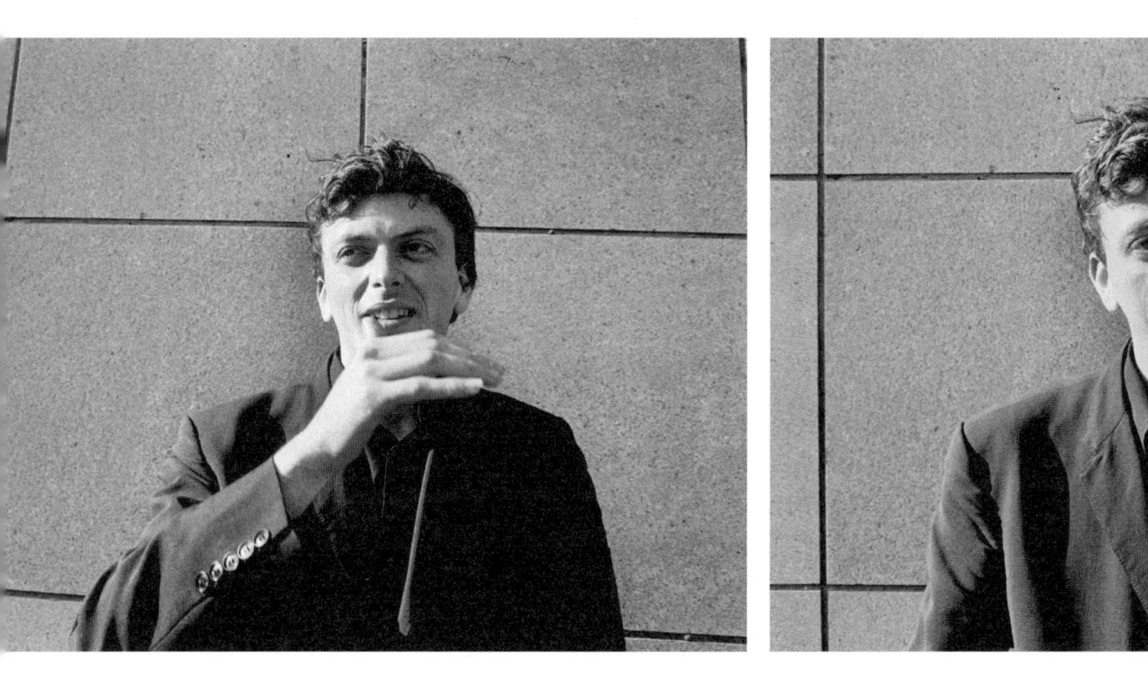

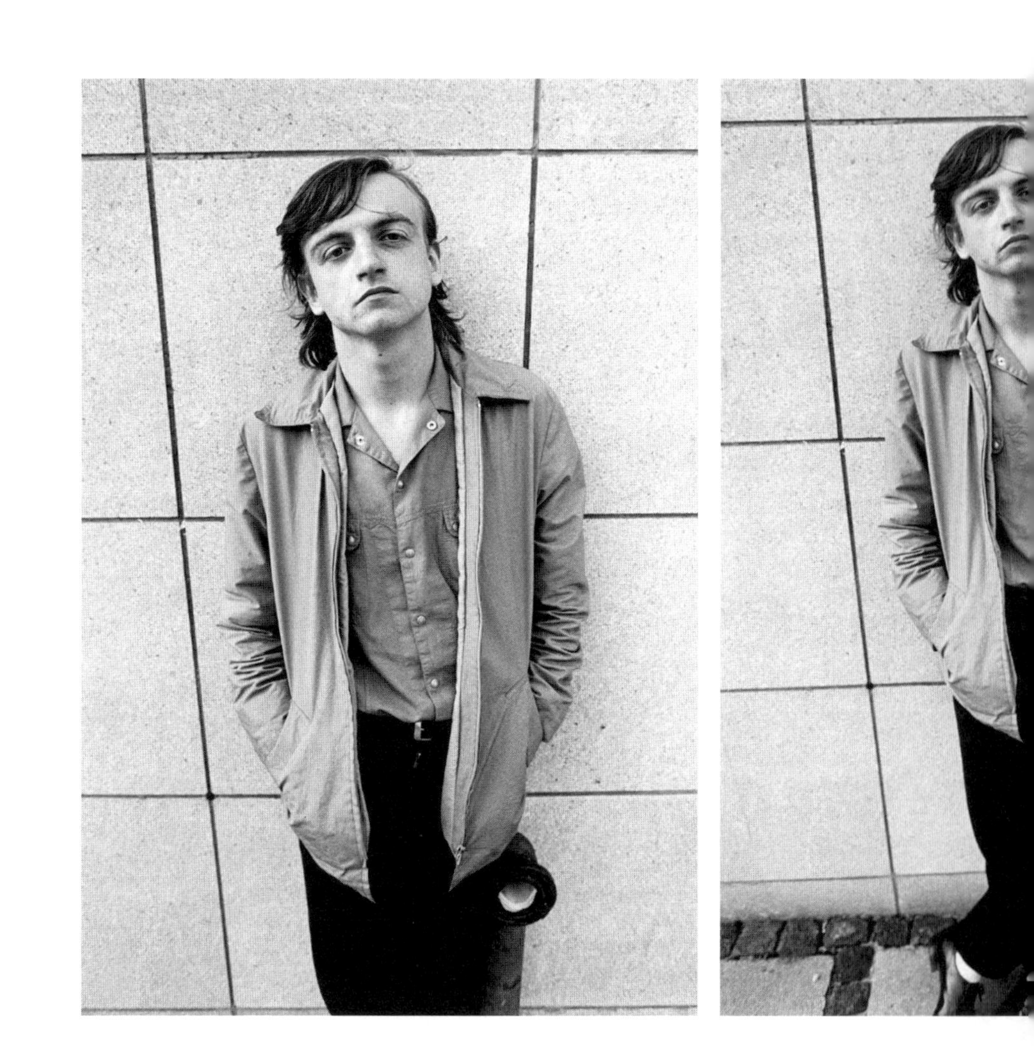

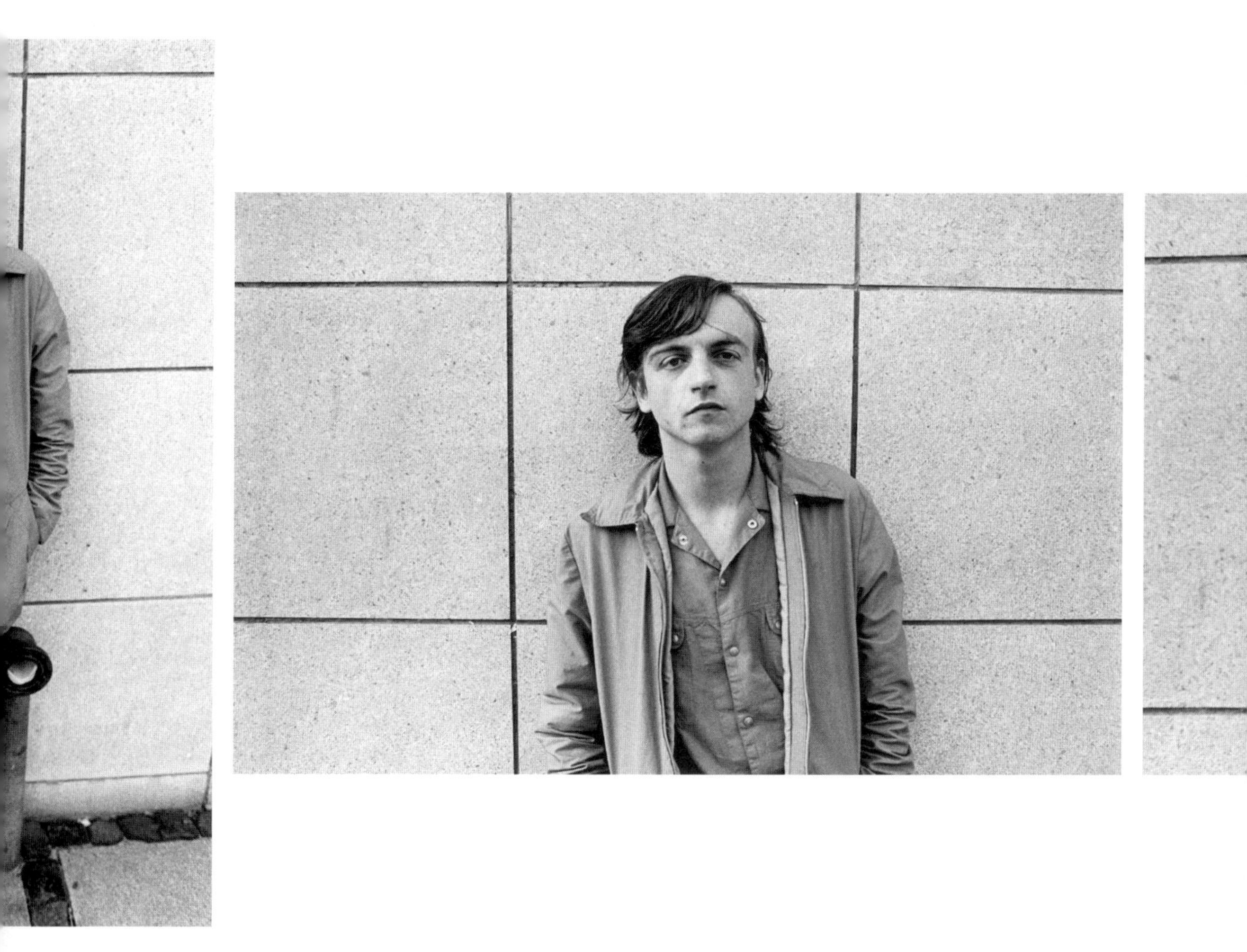

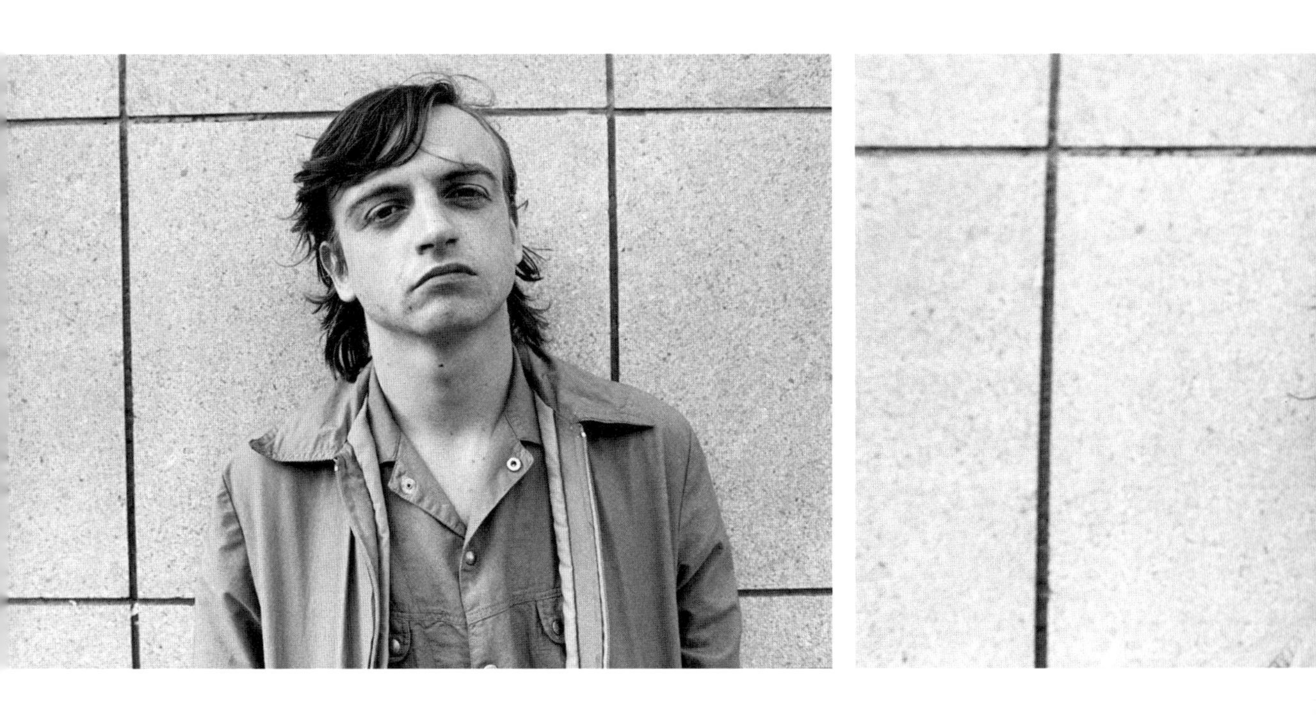

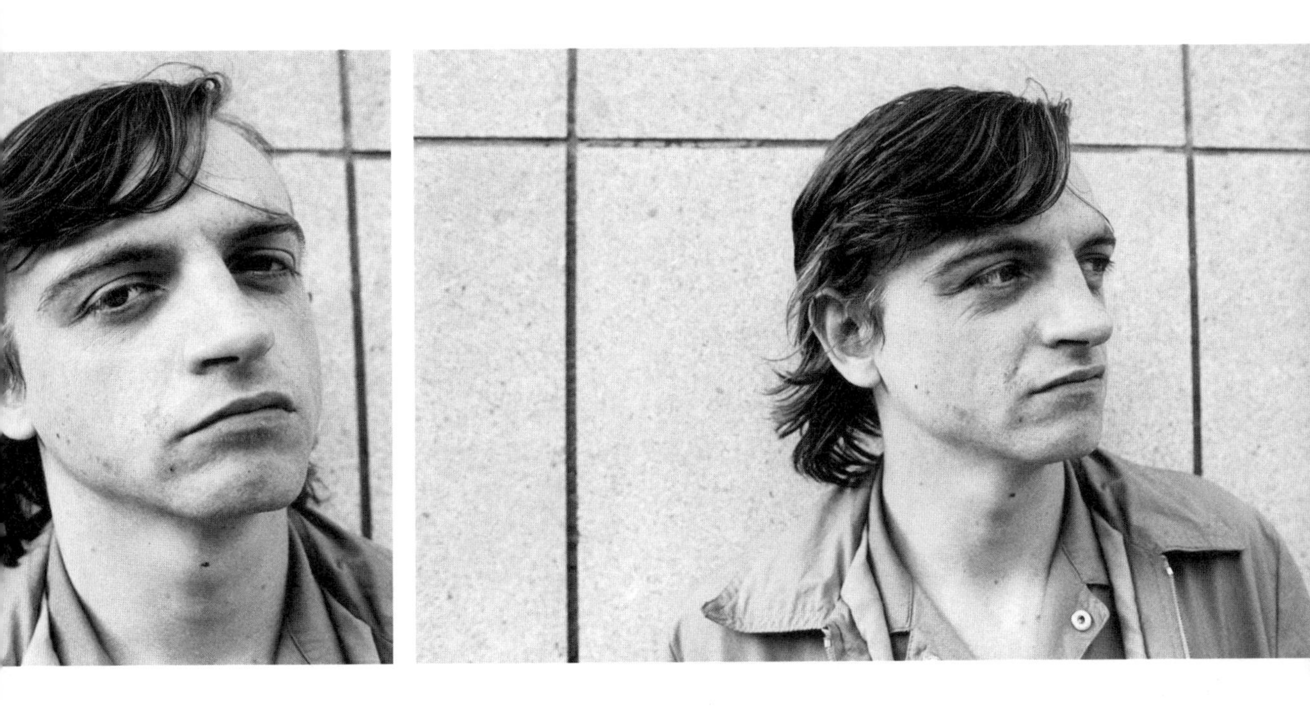

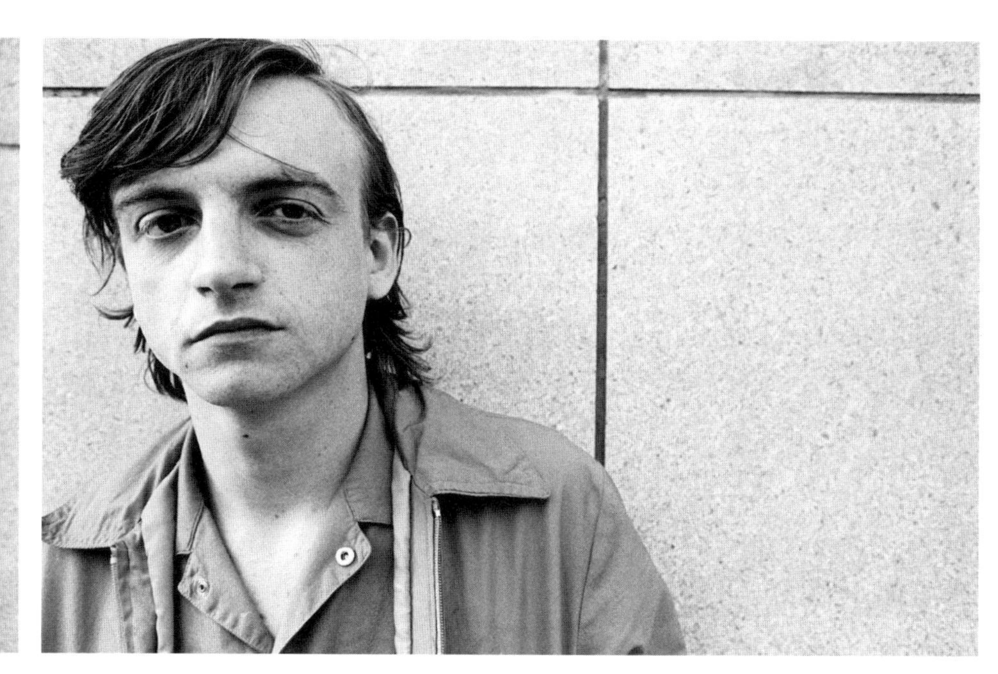

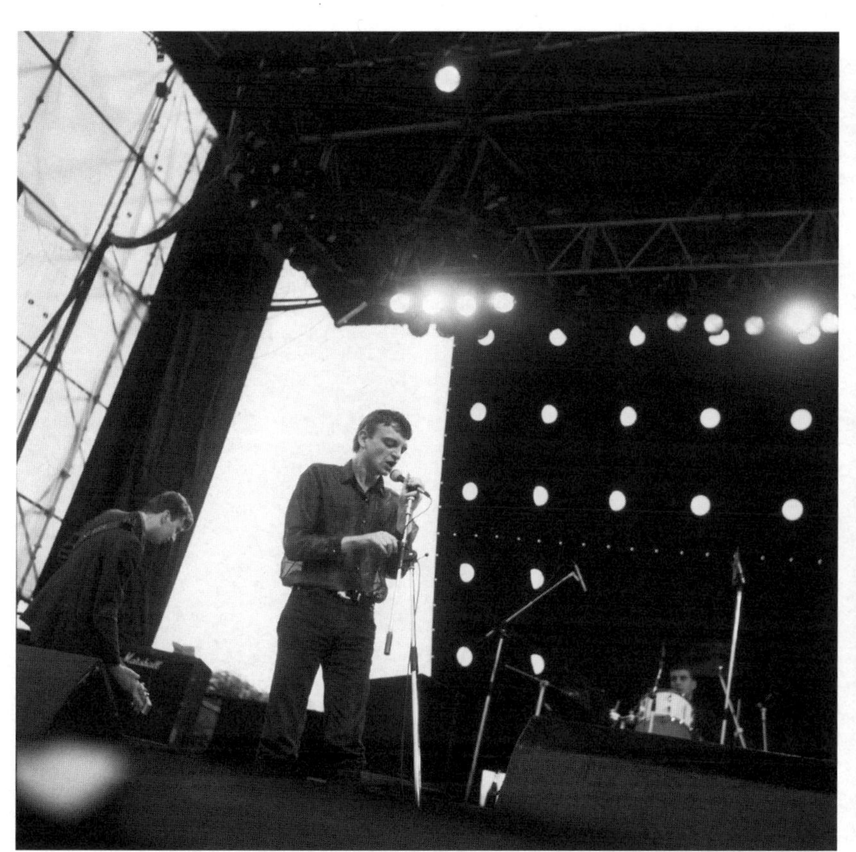
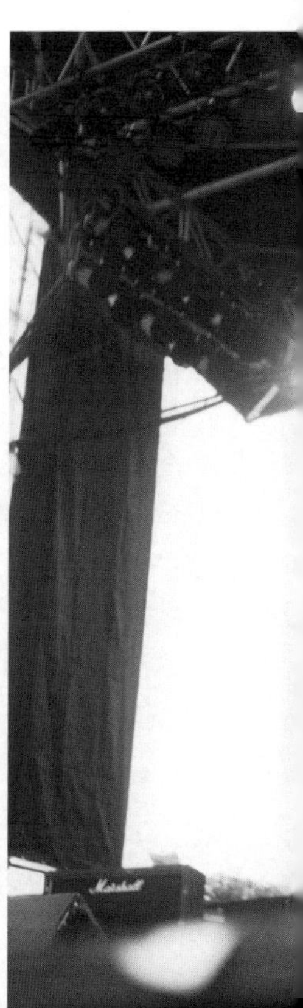

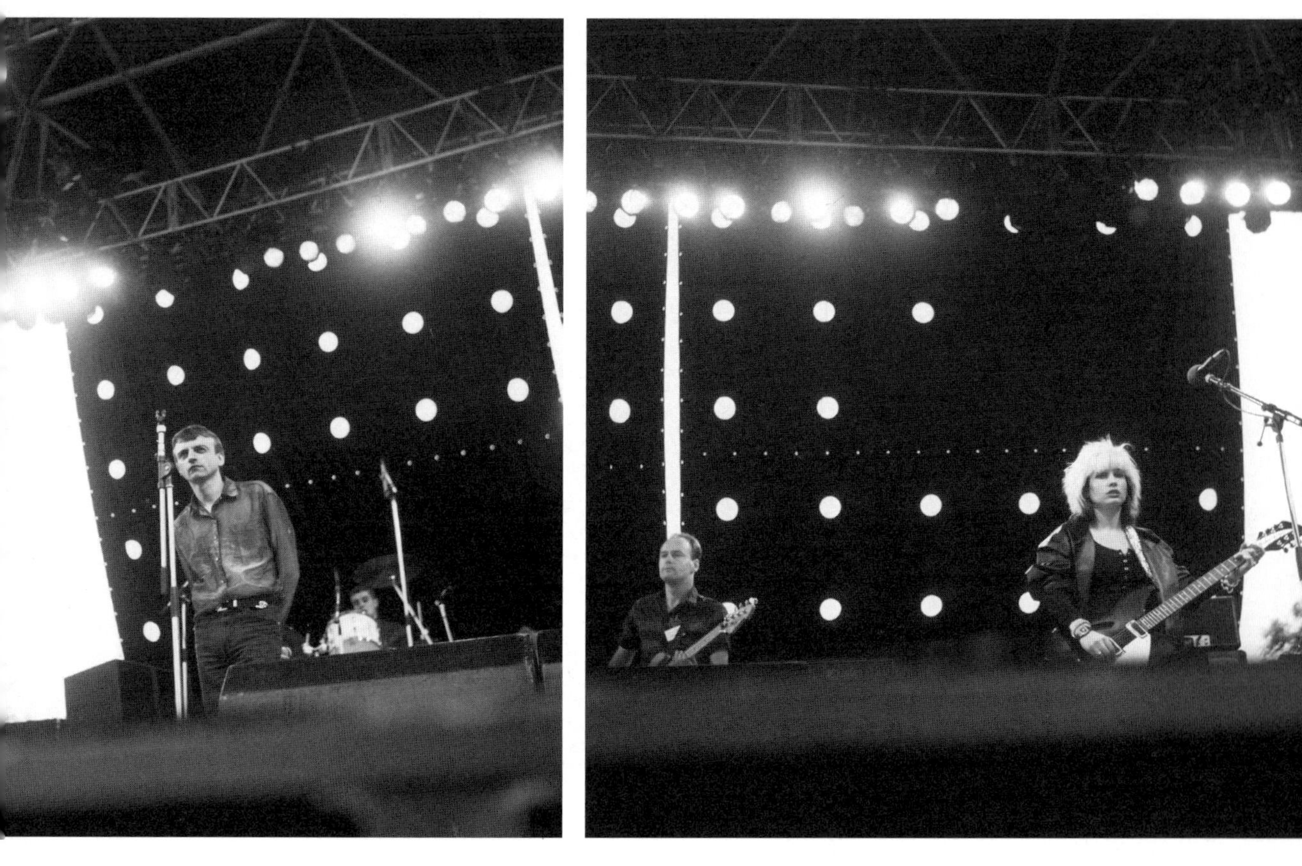

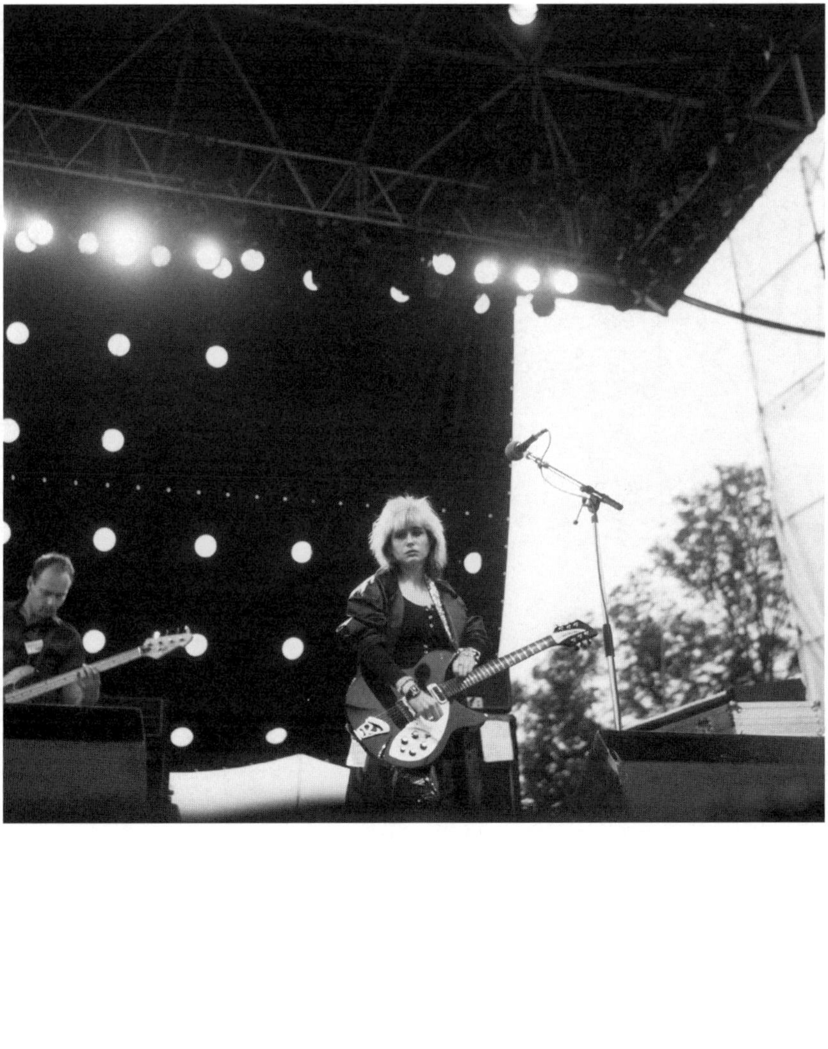

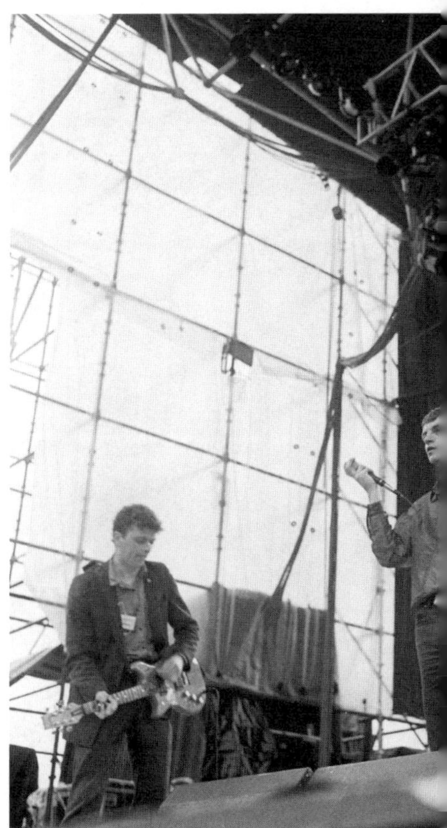

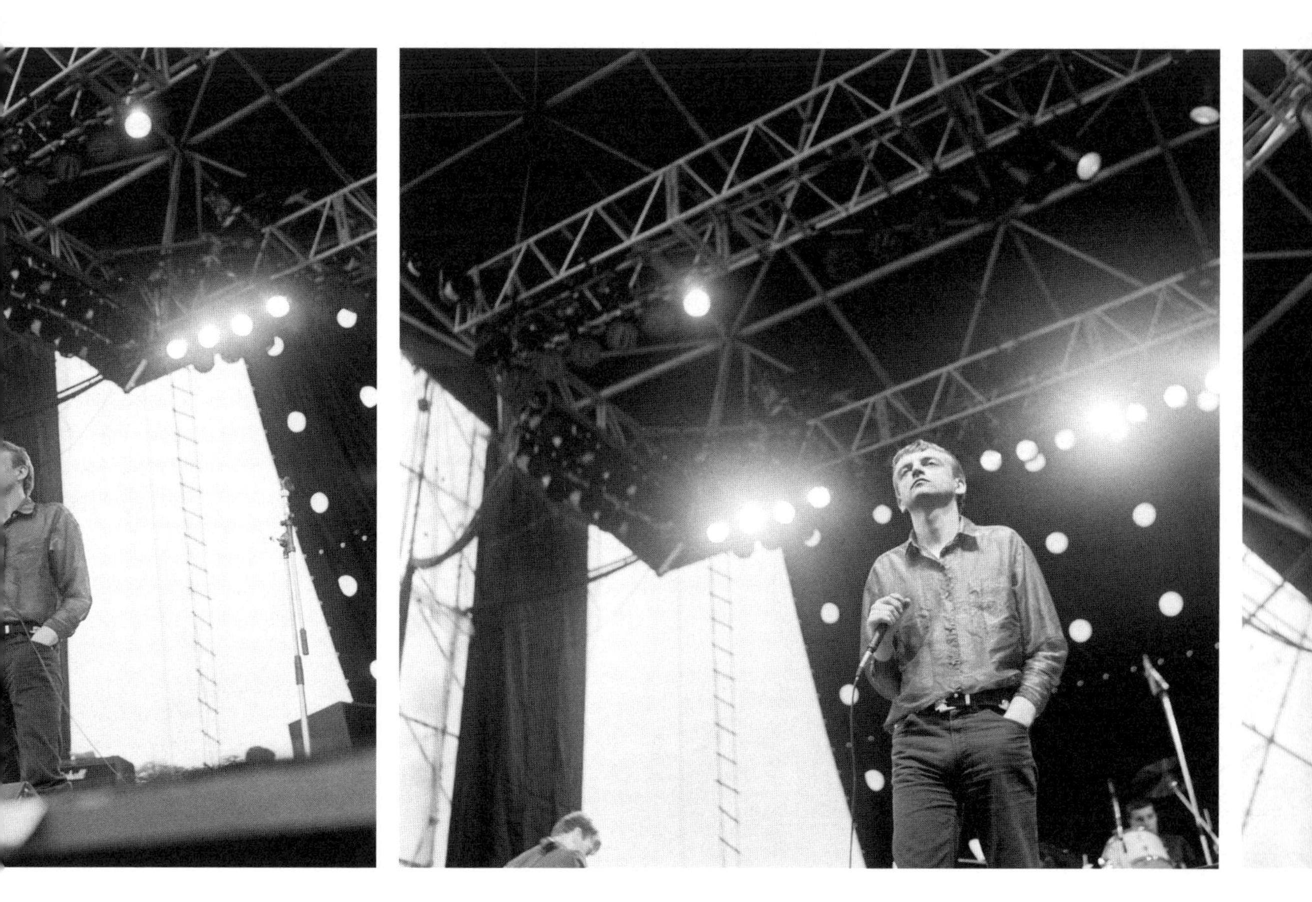

The Fall
(and my camera)

by Lars Schwander with Michael Flack

It is a bright clear afternoon as I enter Saltlageret in Copenhagen. A former municipal hall that used to store road salt for city streets, now it's a place for concerts, smelling of dust, old beer and urine. The hall is almost empty. I take a chair and put it out on the middle of the floor, right in front of the soundman, who along with the bar staff is one of the few people present. The stage is also prepared for the day's rehearsal. I notice the chain of sound from amplifier to microphone, from microphone through cable and into and out of another, larger, amplifier. Looks like a perfect set-up for the clanking, rattling sound of The Fall.

I'm sitting here for a few minutes before The Fall appear on stage. They play a couple of songs before Mark E Smith paces in, grabs a microphone and stalks restlessly back and forth, as if he were a tiger in a cage. He strides back and forth a few times before beginning to recite his lyrics.

A few days earlier, I'd been sitting at home listening to a promo cassette from Rough Trade (Rough Tapes!) with upcoming songs. It's difficult, and somewhat contentious, to talk about a golden age when it comes to The Fall. But from 1980 to 1984 the group releases a series of powerful records, charged and charred and strange and changed: LPs such as Grotesque, Hex Enduction Hour and Perverted By Language, and the incredible mini-LP Slates. And this prolific output is supplemented by a series of startling singles, with character sketches and stories of the strange: How I

Wrote Elastic Man, Totally Wired, The Man Whose Head Expanded, Kicker Conspiracy.

These last two are on my promo tape, one of the happy products of my editorial role with the leading 'punk magazine' Sidegaden, and my writings for various magazines. Sidegaden captures much of the energy of the time including young lyricists, the wild painting (mainly from Germany) and everything of the post-punk kind. At the same time I am working as a volunteer at Dansk Sam, the company for distributing independent music in Denmark. I have access to the latest of everything and everybody on the scene - New Order, who released the Power Corruption & Lies album in 1983 as well as their epochal Blue Monday single, Scritti Politti's Songs to Remember, Young Marble Giants' Colossal Youth, the Blue Orchids, The Go-Betweens, Aztec Camera! Plenty of records under my arm and on my shelves: reggae, ska, even the British pop-singer Sandie Shaw. Young Marble Giants break up, but we have their offshoot groups, Weekend and Gist, who begin the burgeoning pop-jazz scene in London.

As I'm seated almost alone in Saltlageret, watching and listening to The Fall, there is no mistake about the band: the group *is* Mark E Smith. He is The Fall. I do not know how many members have been in and out of this project – and how many will subsequently come over – but some calculations put the figure at close to 70. The impetus for constant change generating creative renewal, Mark E Smith is the loner and The Fall must follow suit.

Smith is more poet than singer. He recites his lyrics to the sound of this hard-pumped, rattling orchestra that plays tight, but not always in harmony – not sophisticated but energetic and rough. At this point in their long history, The Fall are a two drummer attack, expanding on the Velvet Underground-cum-Johnny Cash palette of Grotesque with pulsing, arterial basslines and acerbic verses voiced by a goblin up to the best kind of no good. He continues to range restlessly on the stage, hunched over a microphone, frequently facing towards the back of the stage, occasionally slamming his hand down with a discordant stab on a keyboard unstaffed since the eviction of Marc Riley on the previous summer's tour of Australasia. He almost spits out the words, this self-taught working class upstart with the north Manchester accent. He lives and breathes The Fall, without the distractions of celebrity or fame, and will continue to live near his family in unglamorous Prestwich. On stage, during both soundcheck and gig, he wears a curly windcheater and clothing that has seen better times. The Fall lack the profile of Manchester contemporaries Joy Division and New Order, but in return they have an almost cult status amongst their followers, a closed company you're only permitted to enter when you understand the greatness of Mark E Smith.

I do not have the set list from June 19th 1983 in Copenhagen. But at the gigs around that time The Fall play *Ludd Gang, Wings, Kicker Conspiracy*, and tracks from the forthcoming <u>Perverted by Language</u> album. There is a huge, trapped aggression about this sound, and Smith doesn't look up from the floor as he paces the stage. Not only because of the sound level, but also due to the sustained pulse from the band and Mark E Smith's invective, I'm almost pushed back into the chair after something close to an hour's sound checking. Then the band disappears and after a while Mark comes back and I ask if I can take some photos. Portraits? Outside? And somehow, it turns out that he is very accommodating, yes, almost gracious.

We all go outside, into the daylight, and I look for a spot with a uniform background. I find a wall at the side of the SAS Hotel, but it's not the large single-coloured surface that I'm looking for. There are these cubes behind, the concrete elements of the building,

that somehow give one great rhythmic structure. Like a great Fall track, the structure initially feels like a nuisance, but later I have to admit it has given the images a distinctive language. The photos express themselves, and are of their moment. You never doubt that they came from this session, this time, this place.

They are standing side by side, The Fall. All the musicians, side by side, lined up in front of the camera. Craig Scanlon, Steve Hanley, MES, and the drummers, Steve's brother Paul and Karl Burns. I ask Mark E Smith to take a step forward, pulling him out from the others for emphasis: this is *his* group. I focus on him, so the others are behind, slightly diffuse, and they are less concentrated than Mark, I can tell, who is present in the moment for most of the shots. I'm standing with my Nikon and I expose a roll of film, maybe one and a half, until I feel like I have a shot or two. I wouldn't say the time is squeezed, but spontaneity is important and the musicians don't have a lot of patience.

I must have gone home straight away and developed both negatives and photographs, because I handed Mark the completed set the same night, before or after the concert. He thanks me and congratulates me, calling me the world's best photographer. I know it's probably not true, but it's nice to hear anyway. He looks at things differently, so maybe he's right and I'm wrong. His taste is not always, how should I put it? Clean? Aesthetic? Comme il faut? It tends to be a little grimy, messy, anti-aesthetic – different. Just look at the cover of <u>Hex Enduction Hour</u>.

One October day in 1984, the postman delivers a package at my door. I open it to find the newly-released <u>Call For Escape Route</u> 12 inch EP, the cover featuring my photo of The Fall at the SAS hotel. It turns out this was taken at a crossroads in The Fall's history. On the back cover is a portrait of Mark E Smith's glamorous new wife, Brix, whom he has also now recruited to play lead guitar.

We meet again, The Fall and I, on July 4th 1986. This time at an open air festival in Funen, in the middle of Denmark. There's more time at this occasion, it's less hectic and more relaxed here, and Mark knows my style, so we do a whole session over an hour or so. I am (again) desperately looking for a fairly uniform background, but have to give up and we agree to take the portraits in front of a shed. This time, the strokes and the grain of the wood bother me more than the first time, but I try to get the lines behind to disappear by 'lifting' the musicians slightly away from the wooden slats. Again Mark E Smith is the one who concentrates, whilst the other band members relax a little more. Brix Smith is now a full member of the group and I do her portraits as she looks up and the light of the evening sun falls onto her face. We also take photos in the tall grass that surrounds parts of the festival area.

The group asks for the photos and I forward them, either to Manchester or London. At the end of September, the <u>Bend Sinister</u> LP appears, including my portraits on the back cover and some concert photos on the inner sleeve. Oddly enough, Mark has opted out of using his own portrait for the record. Instead there are a kind of multiplicity of photocopies of another photo of his face, rendered almost unrecognisable on the front cover. To this day I wonder why he didn't use my portrait, because I myself find it beautiful. Perhaps it was too direct or even 'revealing' – or perhaps his relatively anti-aesthetic sense might explain it. Perhaps he was just being typically contrary. The record itself was mastered from a cassette copy that played slightly too fast, in the teeth of protests from the producer John Leckie, who never worked with The Fall again.

We meet again a third, and last, time at the Roskilde Festival on 27th June 1996. But although I'm waiting for their bus to arrive from the airport, there will be no portraits taken this time. Mark had made himself unpopular, as he was apt to do at this time, with some fellow performers and got himself knocked down and out. They took him to the festival all the same, and when he woke up his head was a bloody mess, to the extent that I don't think he will be able to perform. He does, carried through, not for the first time recently, by ex-wife Brix (recently returned to the group) and the other stalwarts.

The 1983 portraits have an afterlife. I don't know whether these photos are the best of the group – hardly! And I don't have anything to do with it, really. But that afternoon's images will appear again and again in many possible and impossible contexts. And when the internet is born, they are diligently distributed. The American artist Tony Oursler visits me some years later and is surprised to find in passing that I took them.

Mark E Smith's health falters, after many more records and fights and concerts and just the occasional cancelled show, but he battles through his cancer treatments to perform from a wheelchair through the autumn of 2017. When he dies, on 24th January 2018, in Prestwich, just north of Manchester, where he lived most of his (short) life, someone makes posters out of the 1983 portraits and hangs them up on the local lampposts. His last partner, Pamela Vander, asks whether she can use my portrait from that time for the funeral? It stands inside the church and is printed on the front of the order of service.

I feel it's a strange story that these pictures have gone through, a fate I could not have foreseen. I know that photographs retain only the moment in which they were made, and that only time and circumstances render them historic. I did not imagine, standing with my Nikon outside Saltlageret in the clear Danish daylight of July 1983, that that session would still be remembered at the close of The Fall's story.

Lars Schwander — The Fall (and my camera)

First Edition, Second Printing 2025
© 2019 Lars Schwander & At Last Books

Text by Lars Schwander and Michael Flack
Edited by Lars Schwander & Hans Munk
Designed by Hans Munk

Printed by Frederiksberg Bogtrykkeri
Set in Junicode

Published by **At Last Books**
www.atlastbooks.com

ISBN: 978-87-999667-8-3

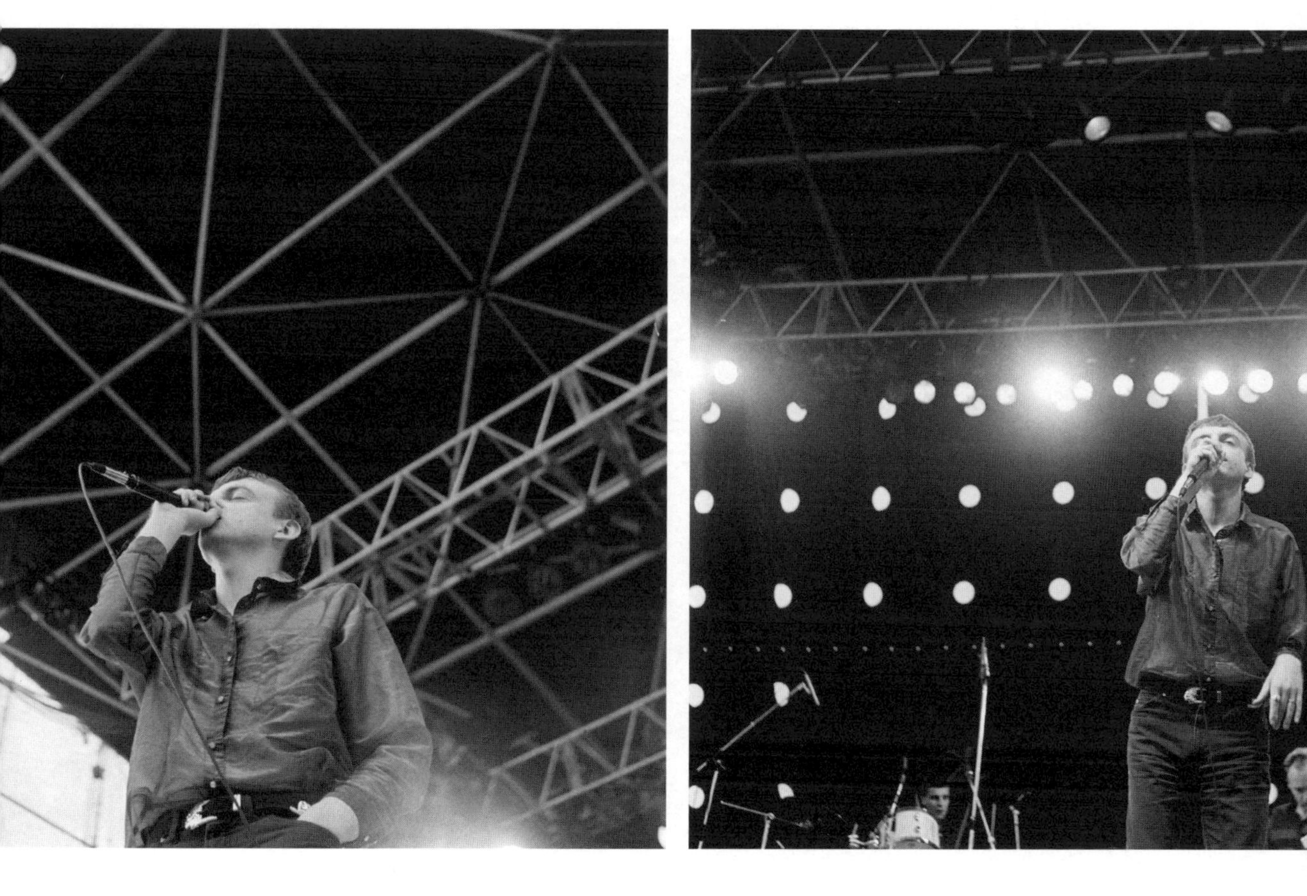

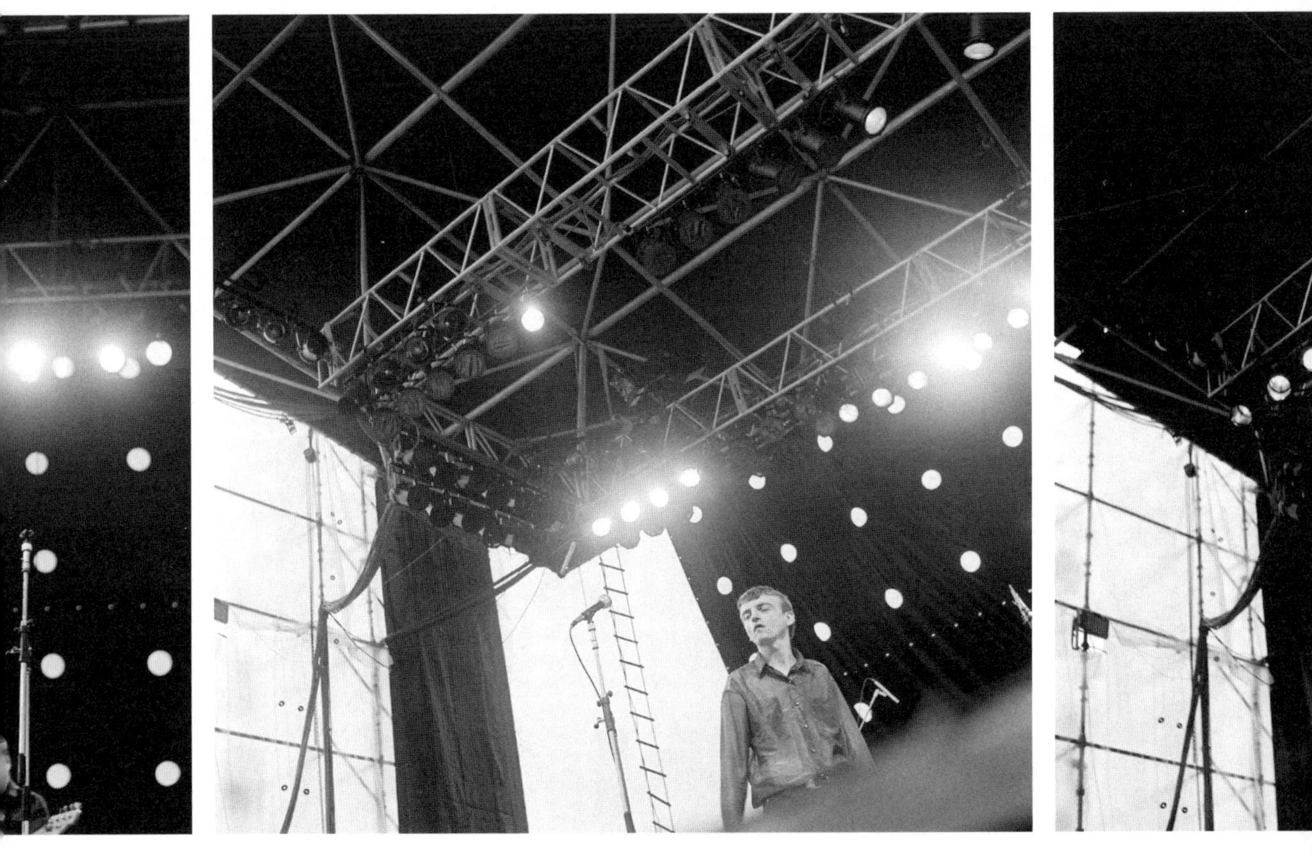

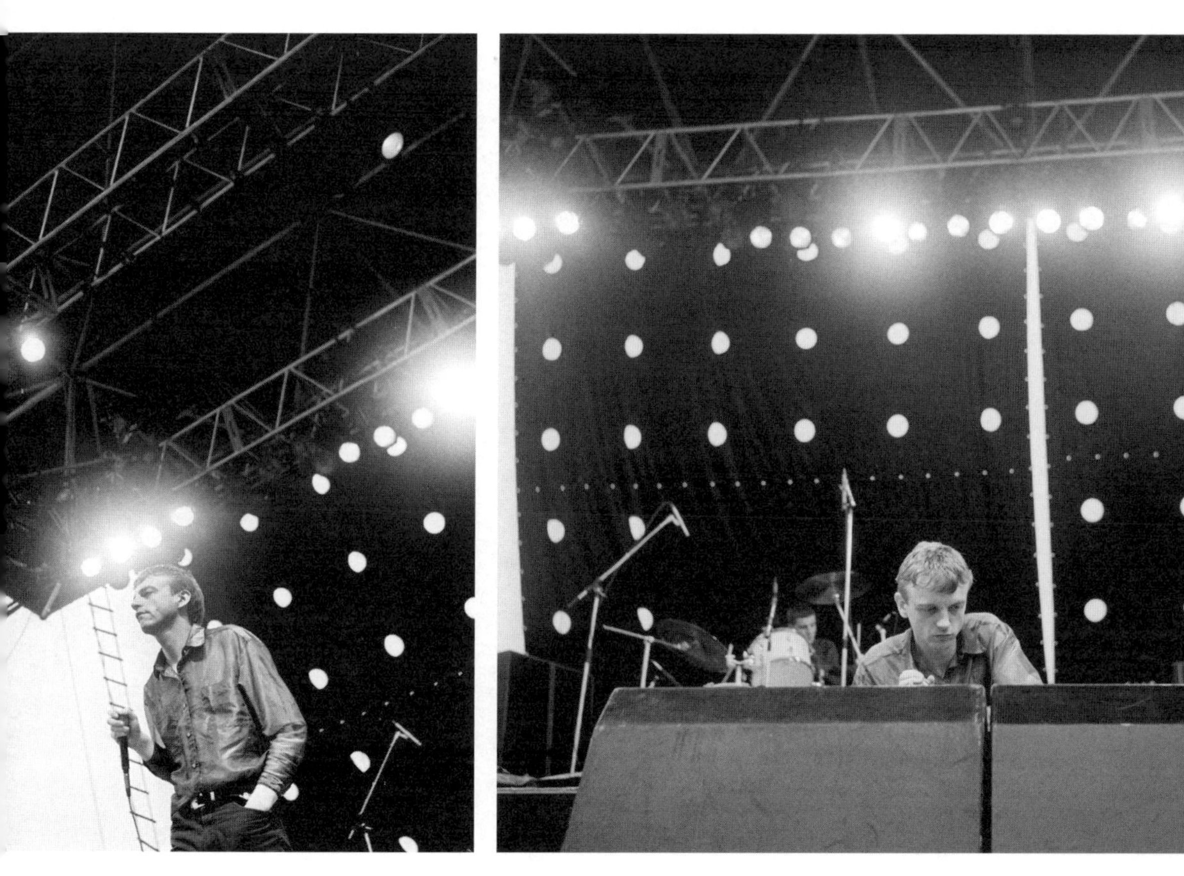

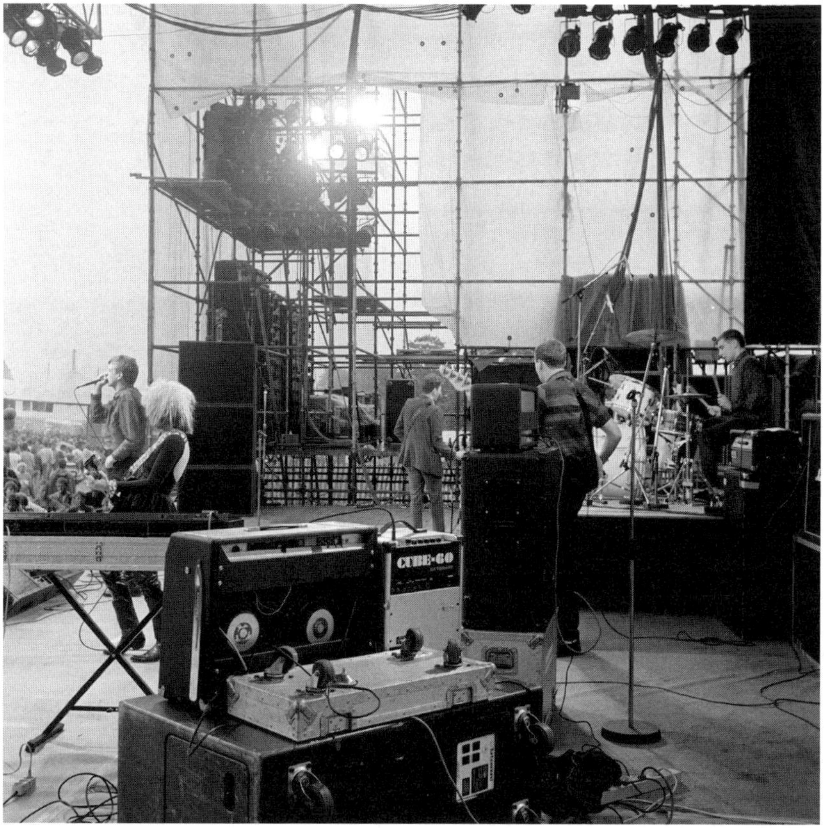

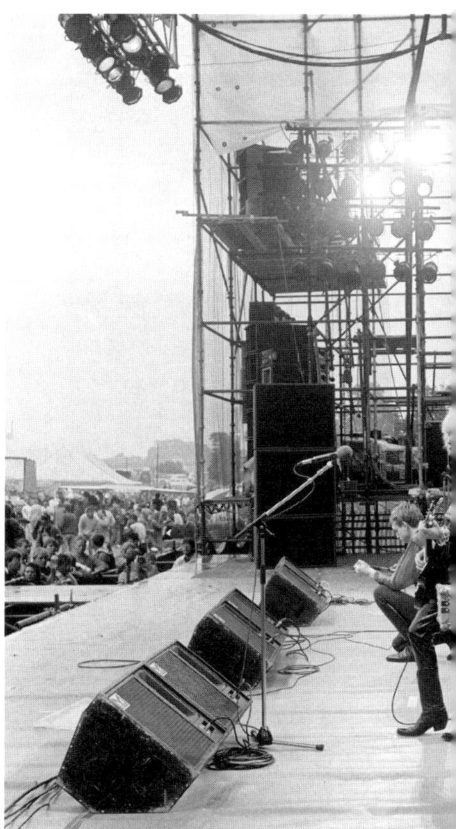

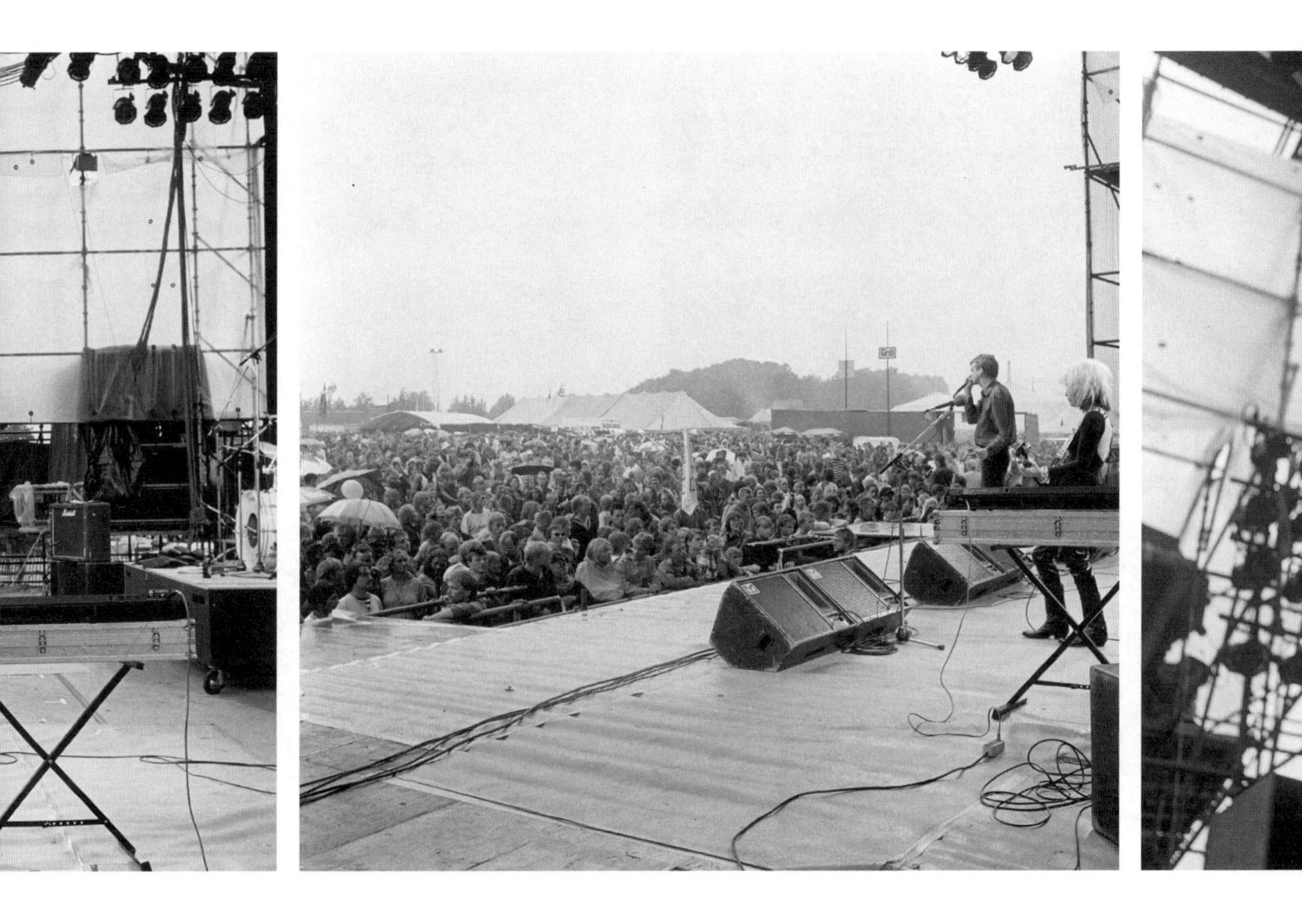

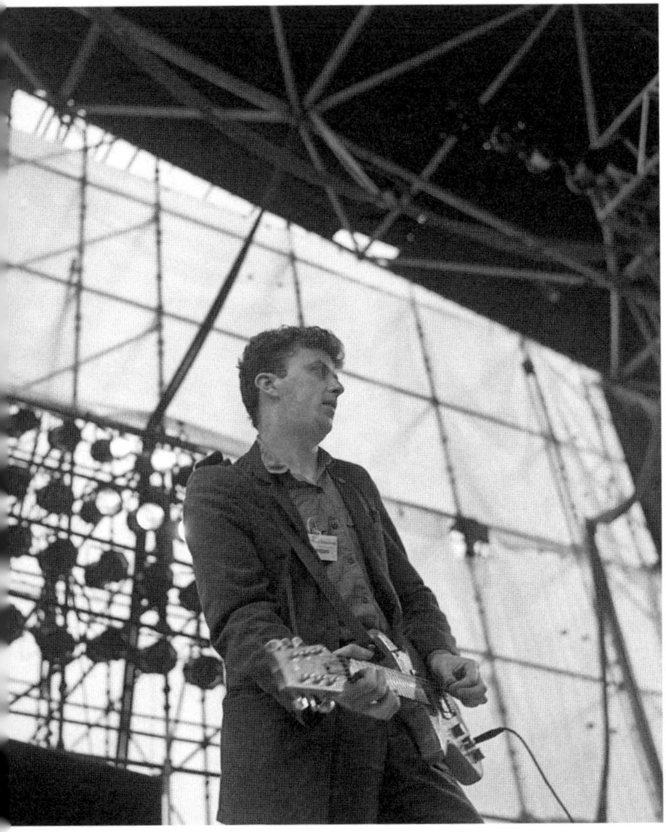

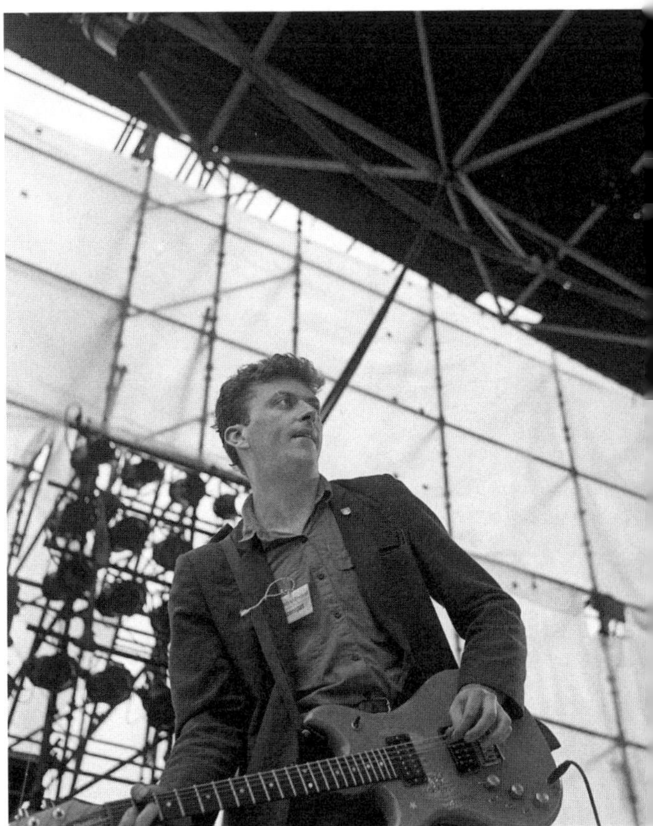

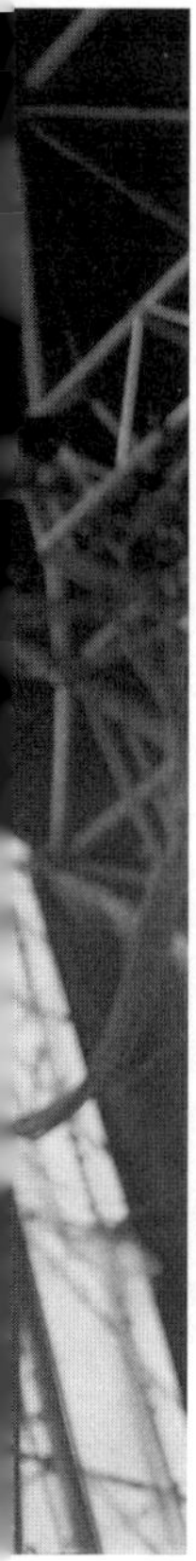

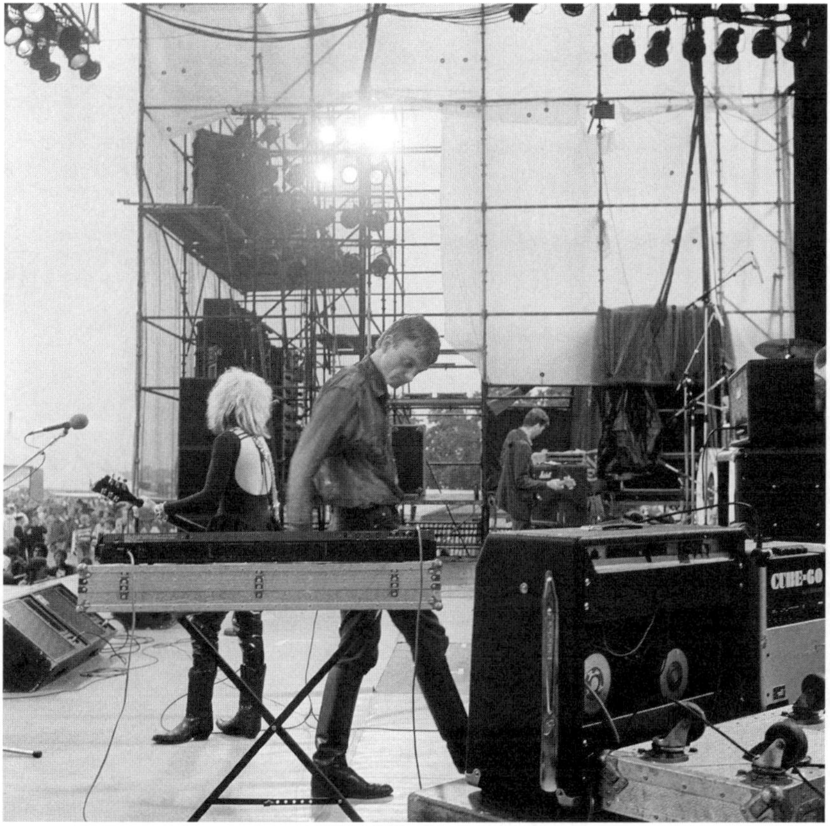

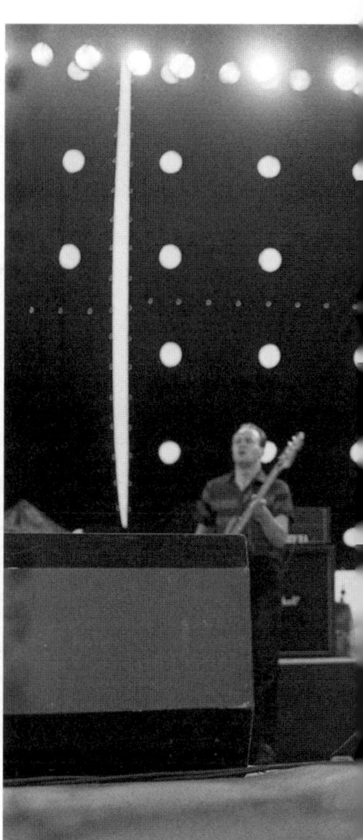

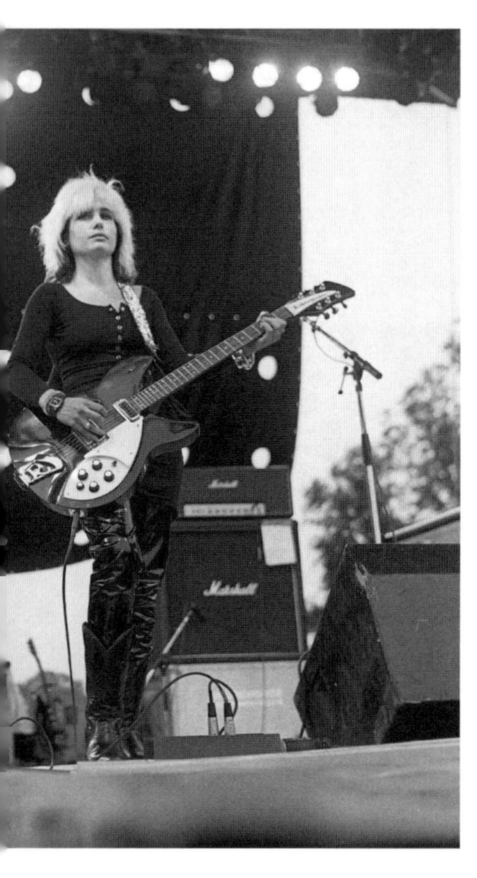
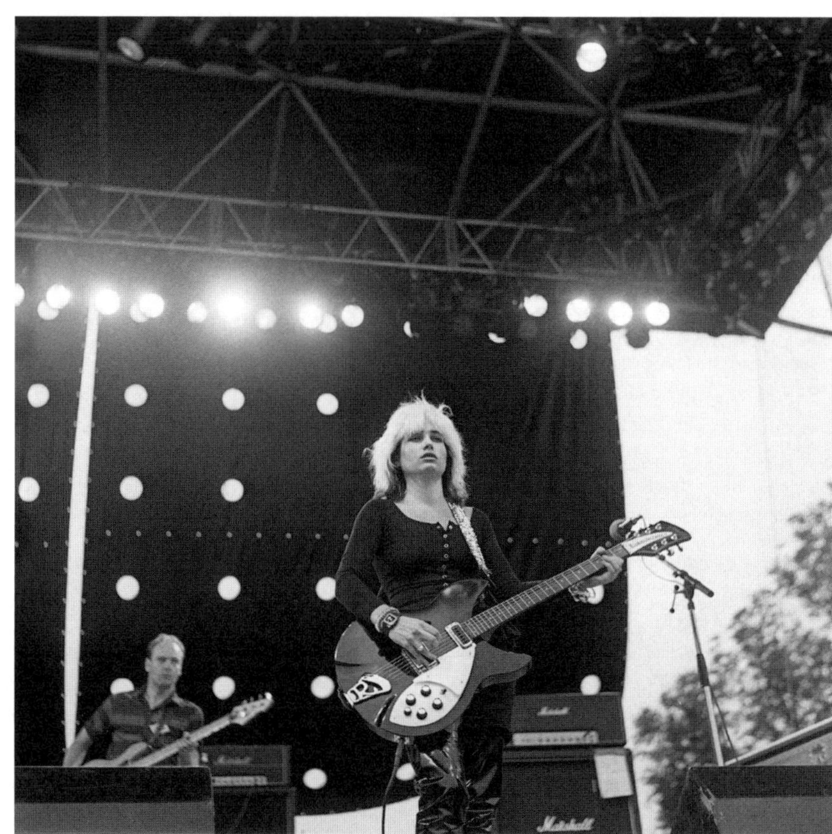

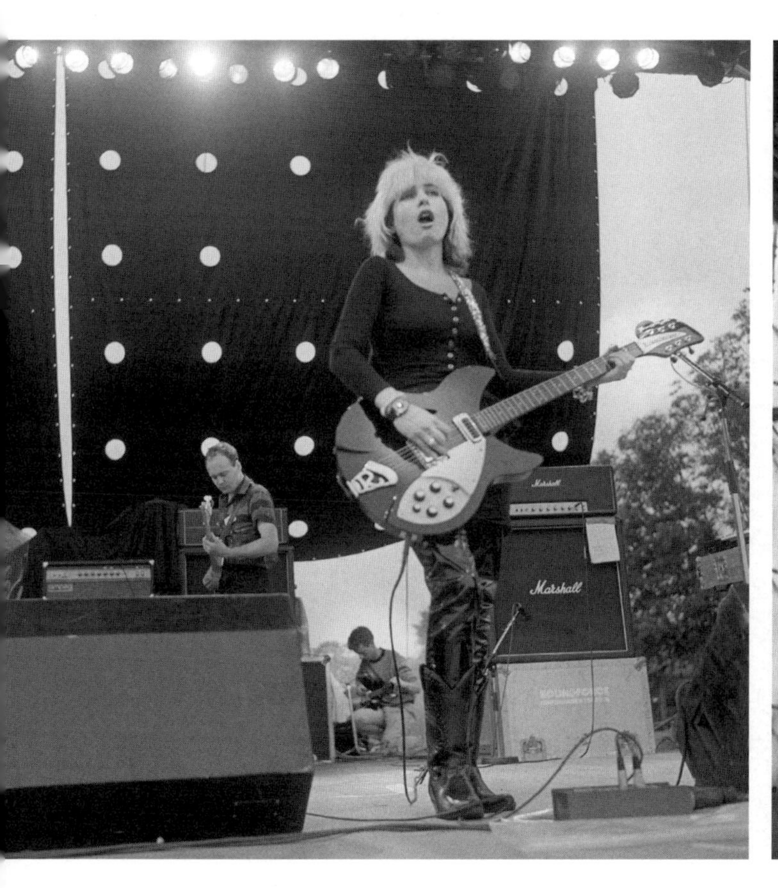
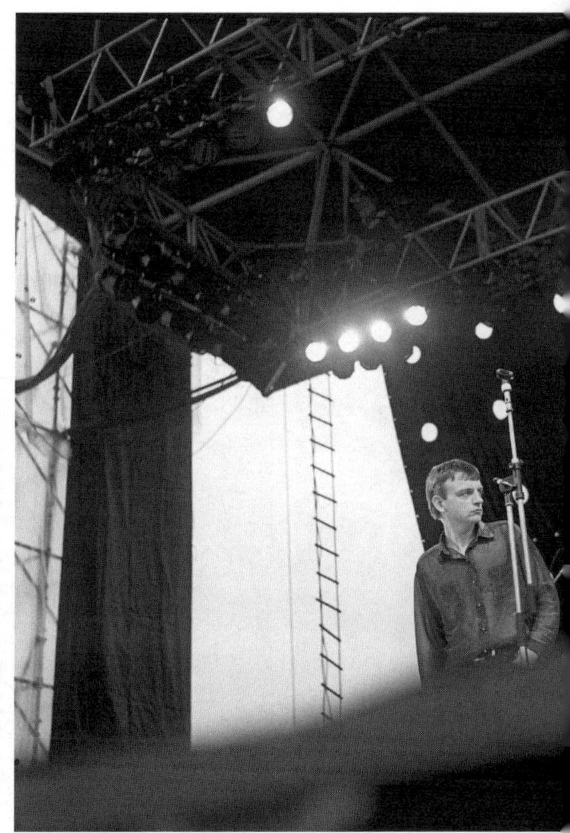

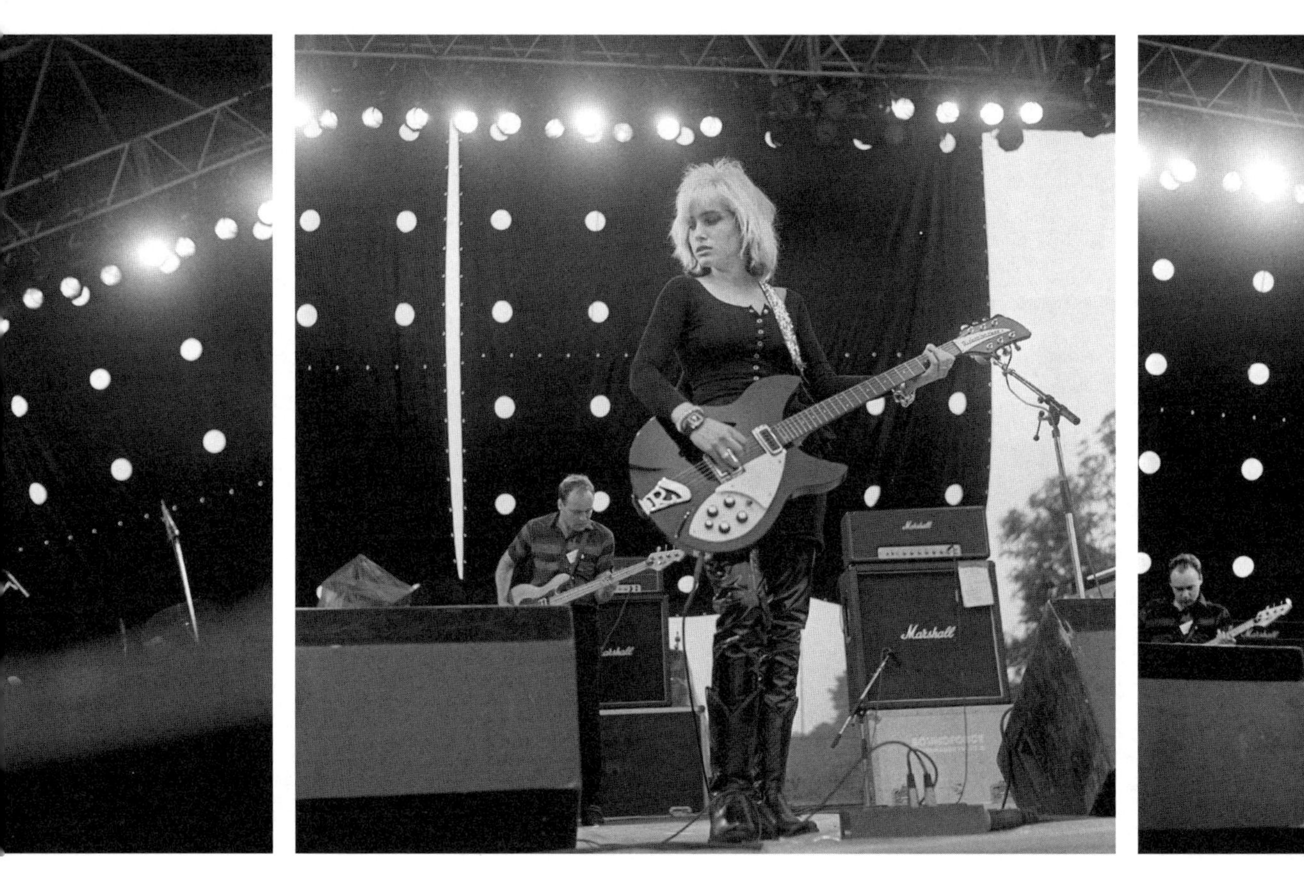

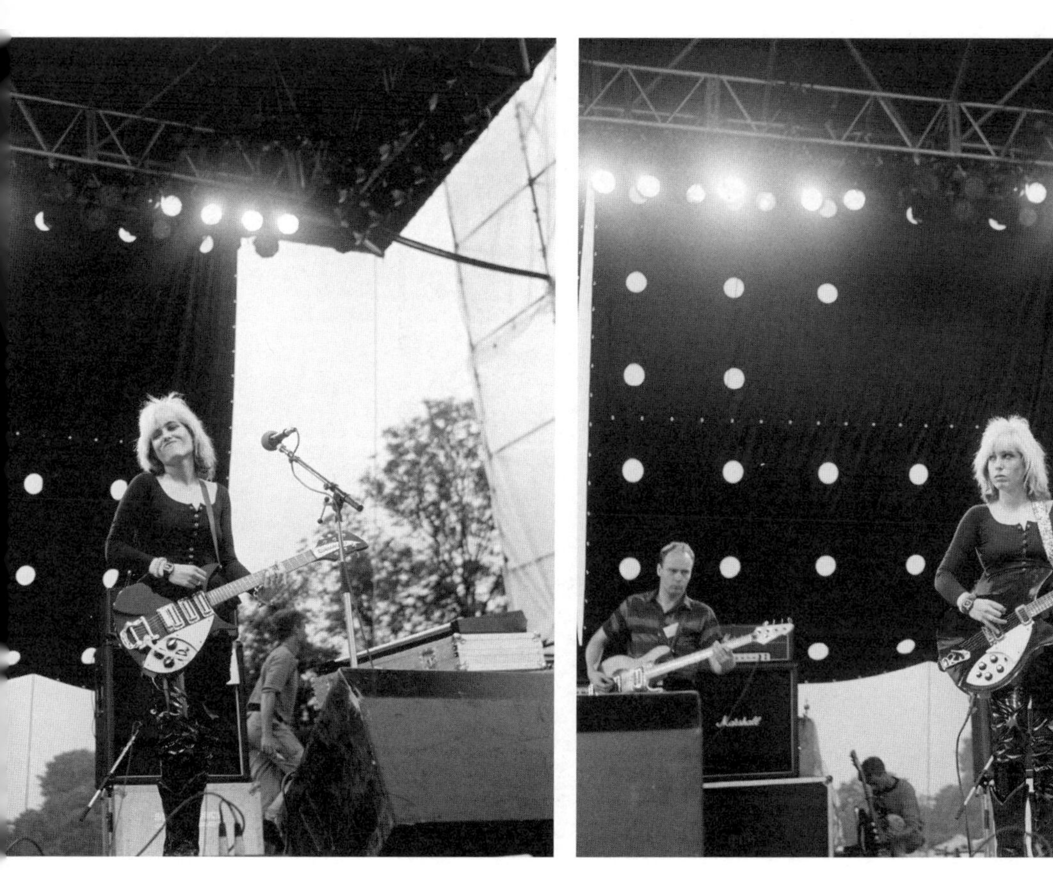

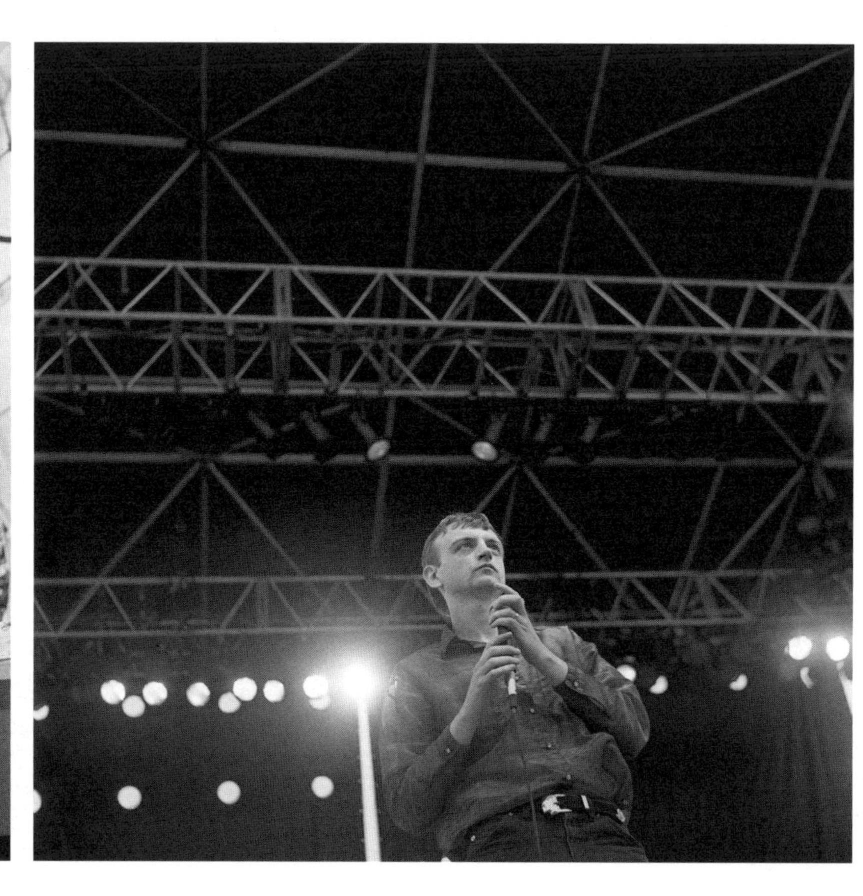

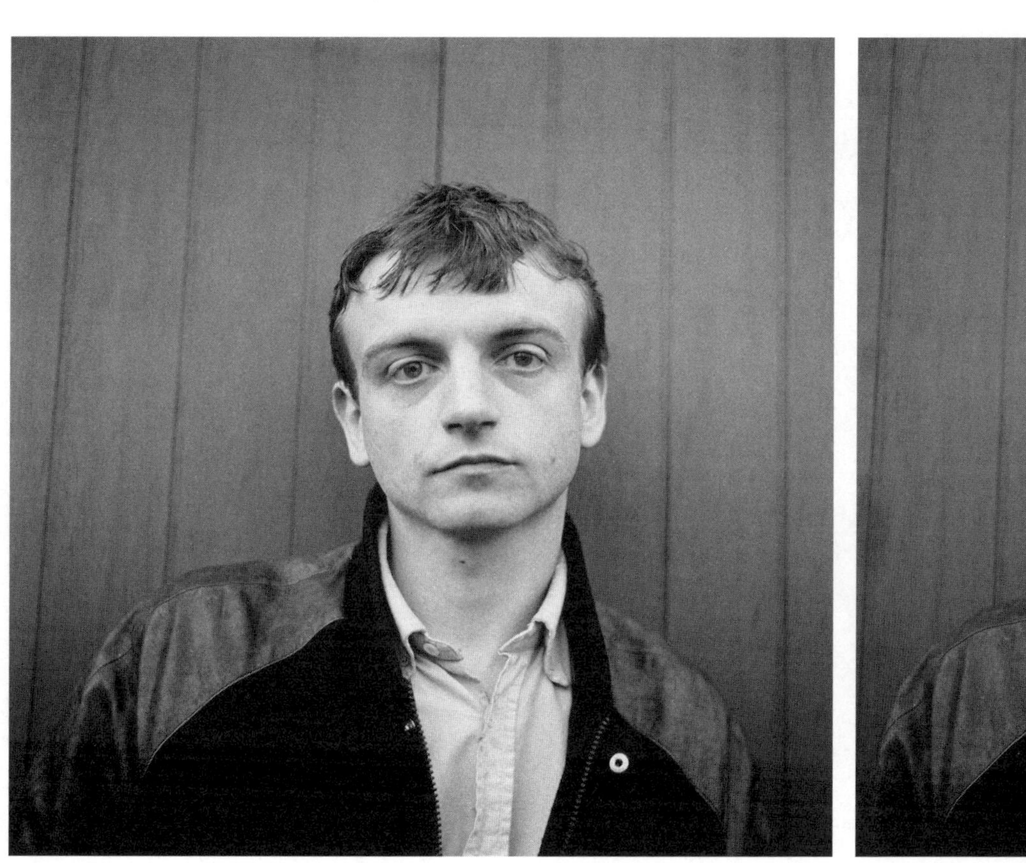

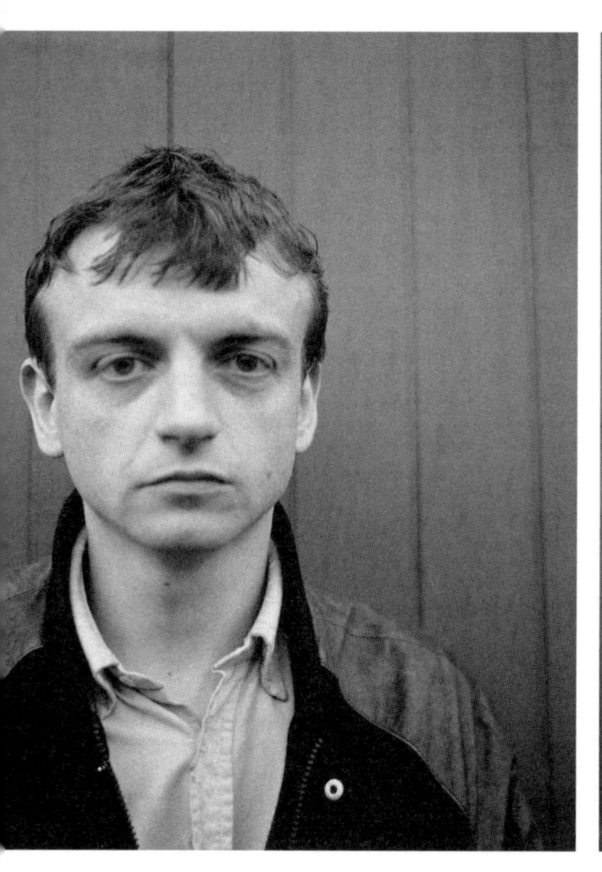
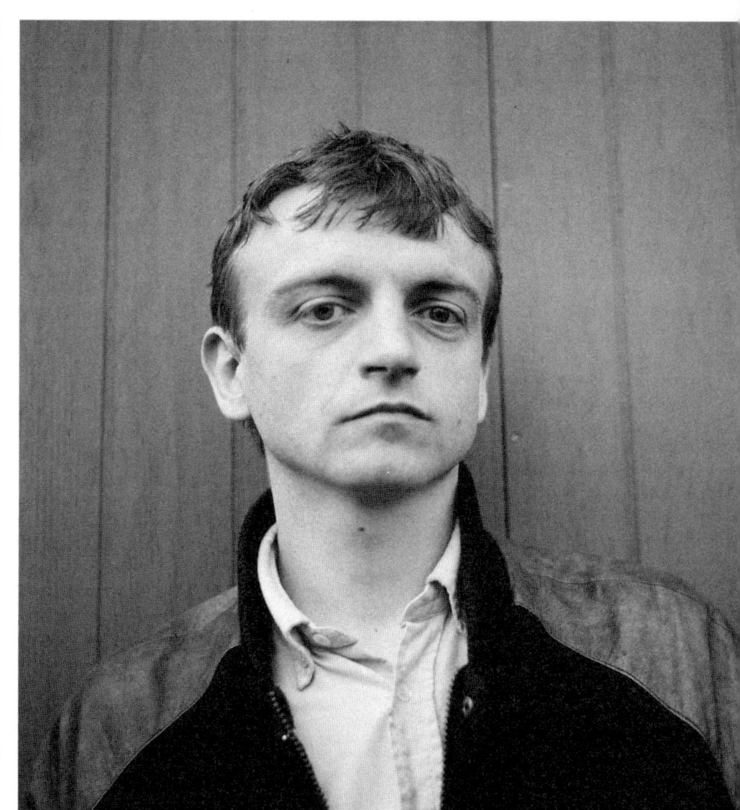

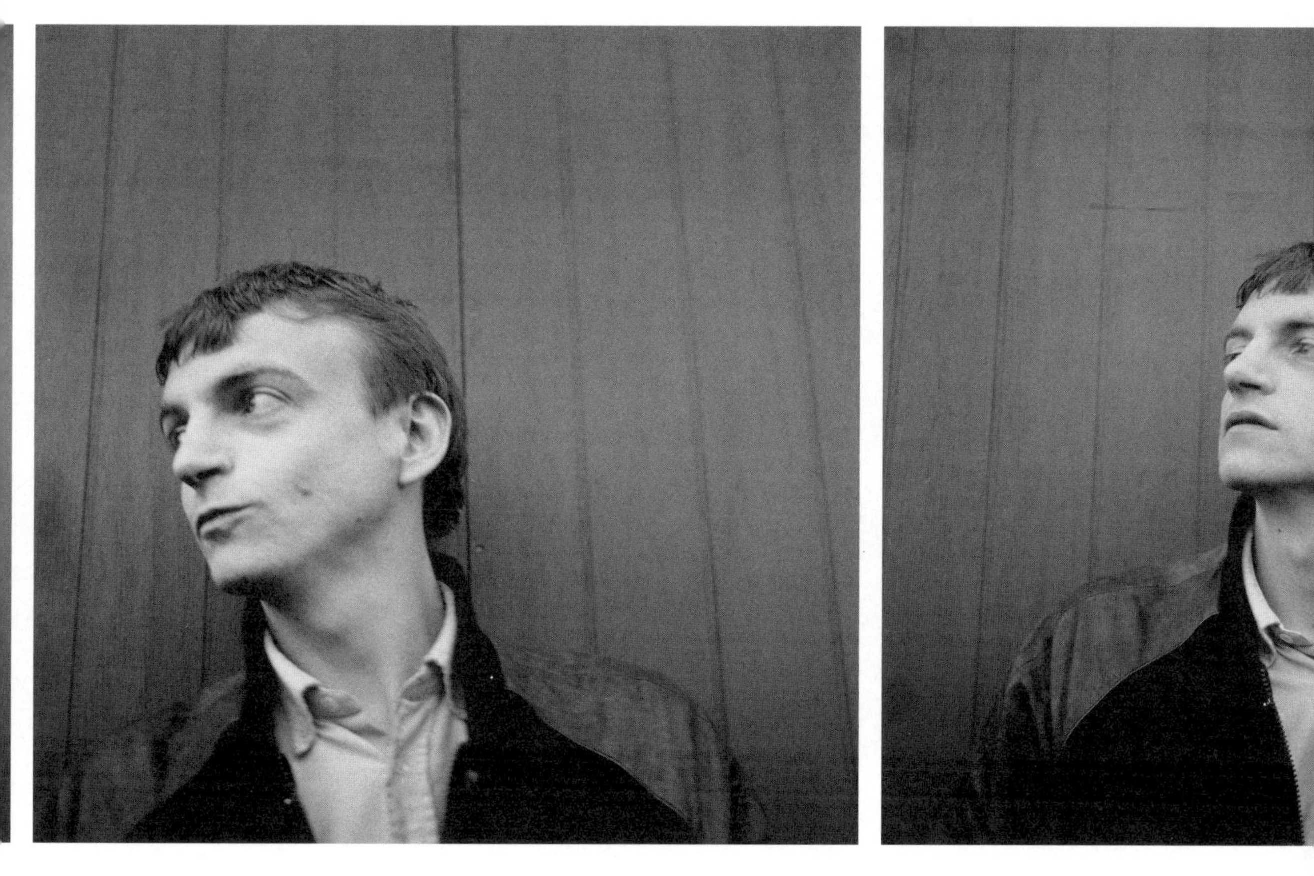

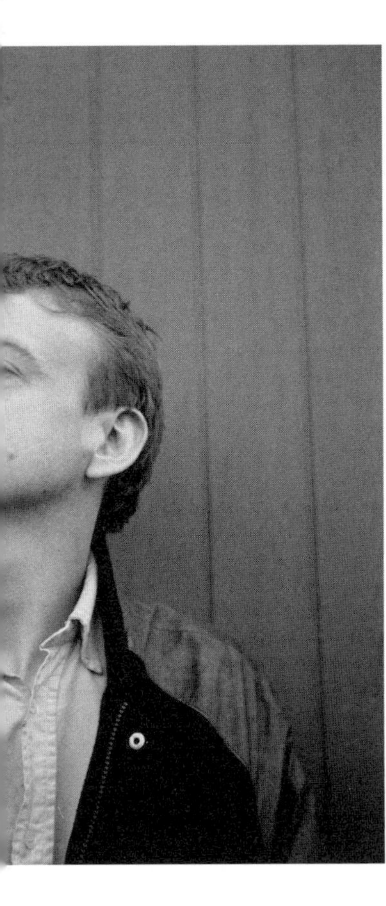

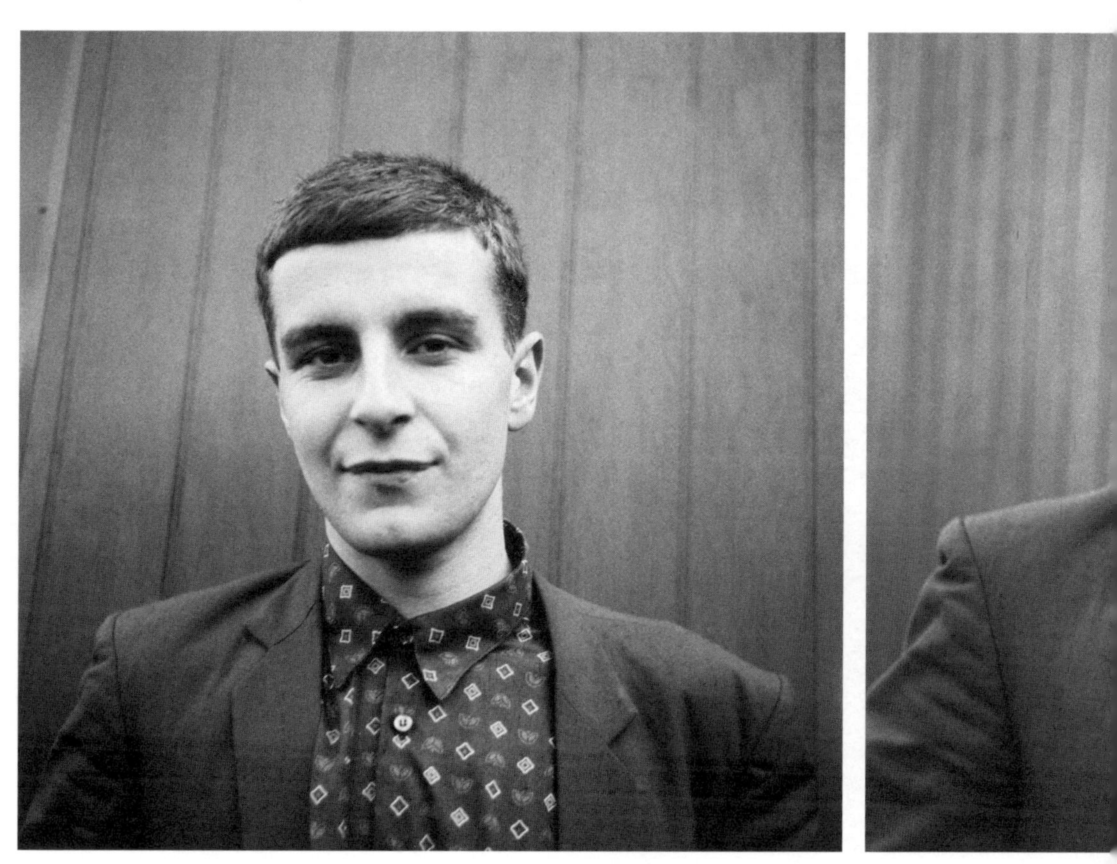

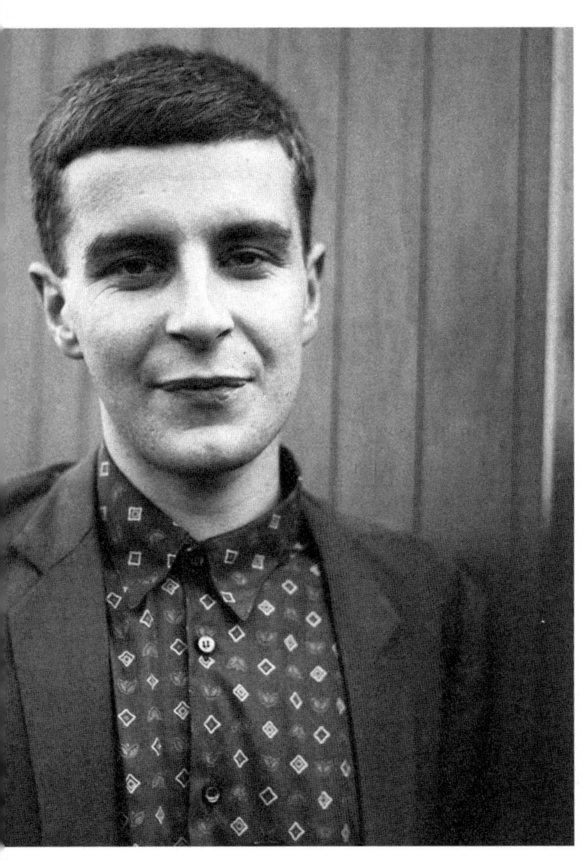

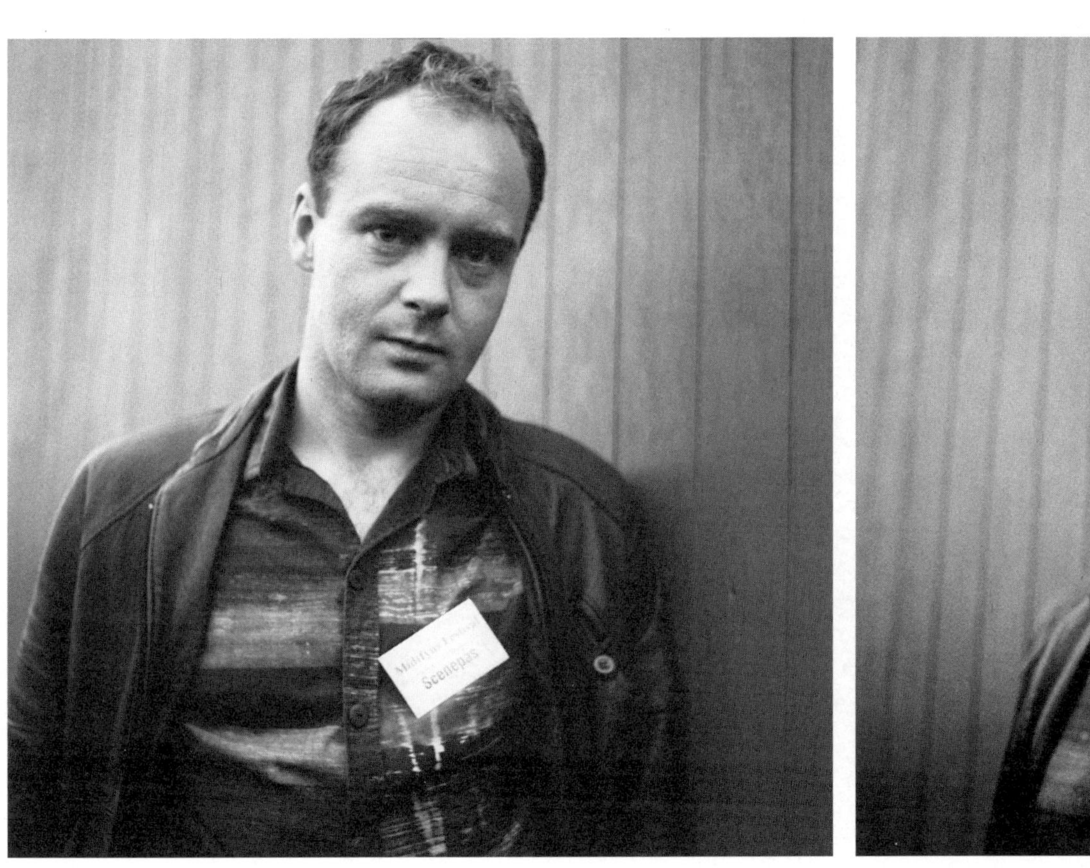

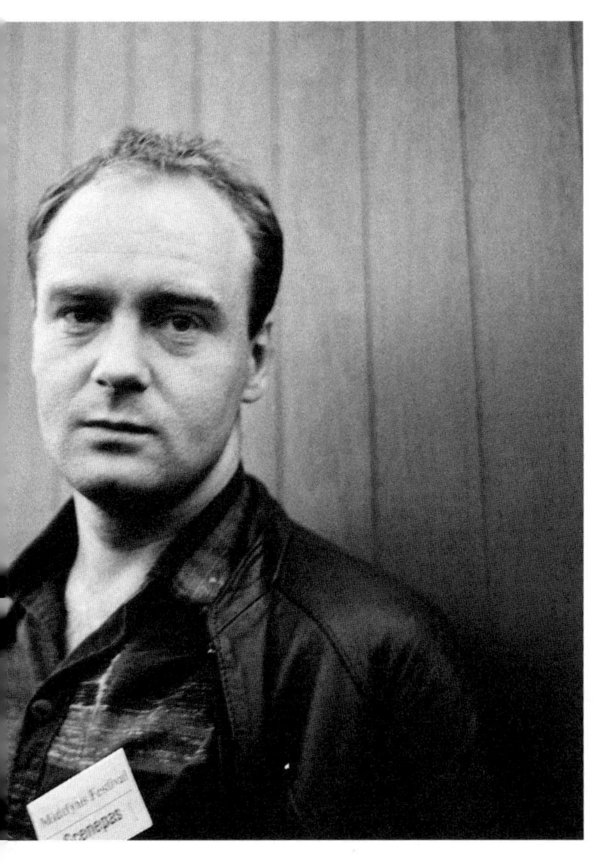
Maerz Festival
Crepas

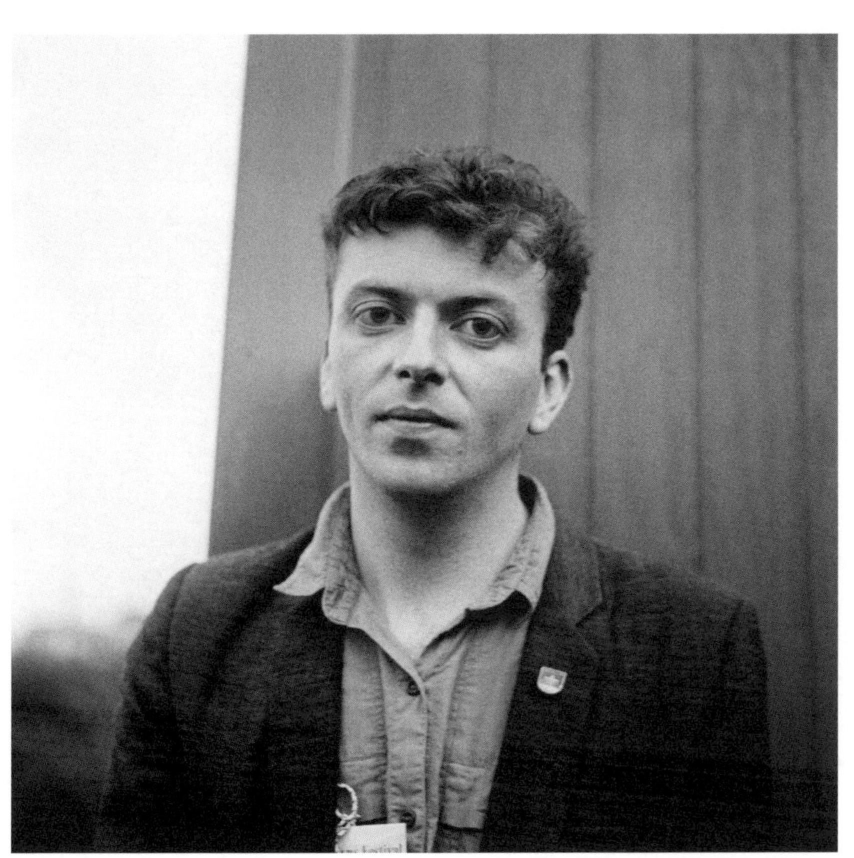

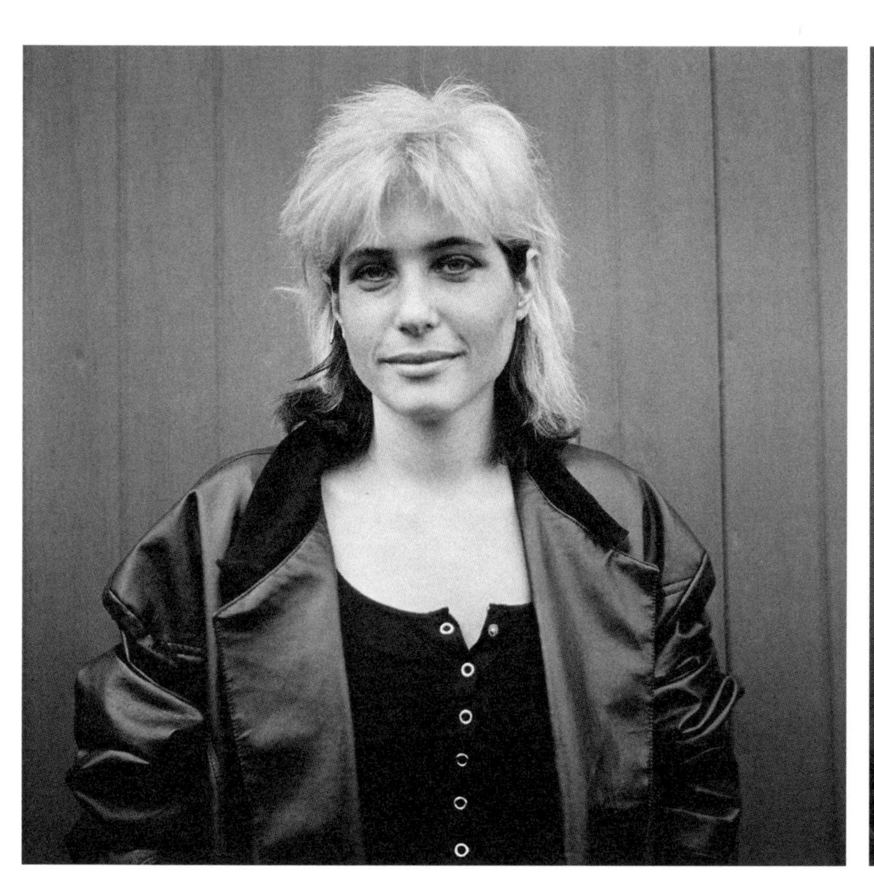

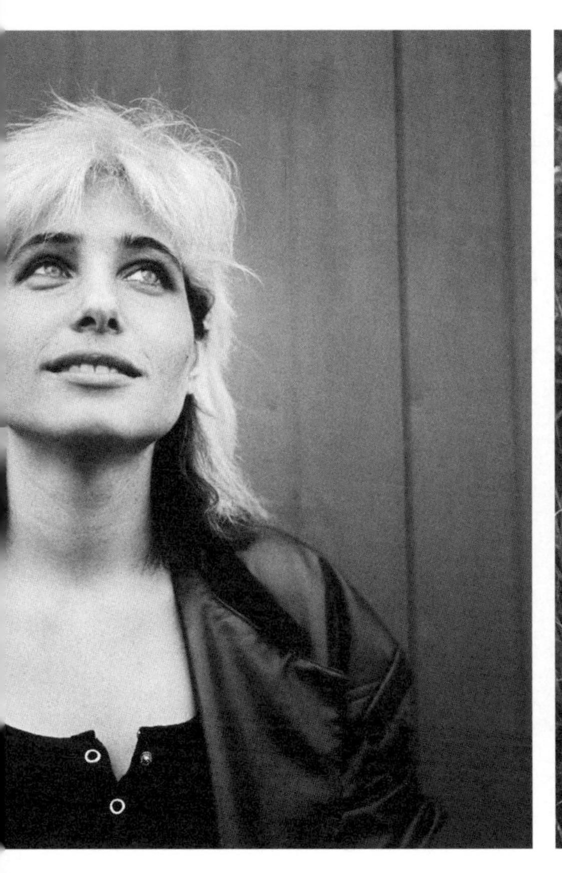
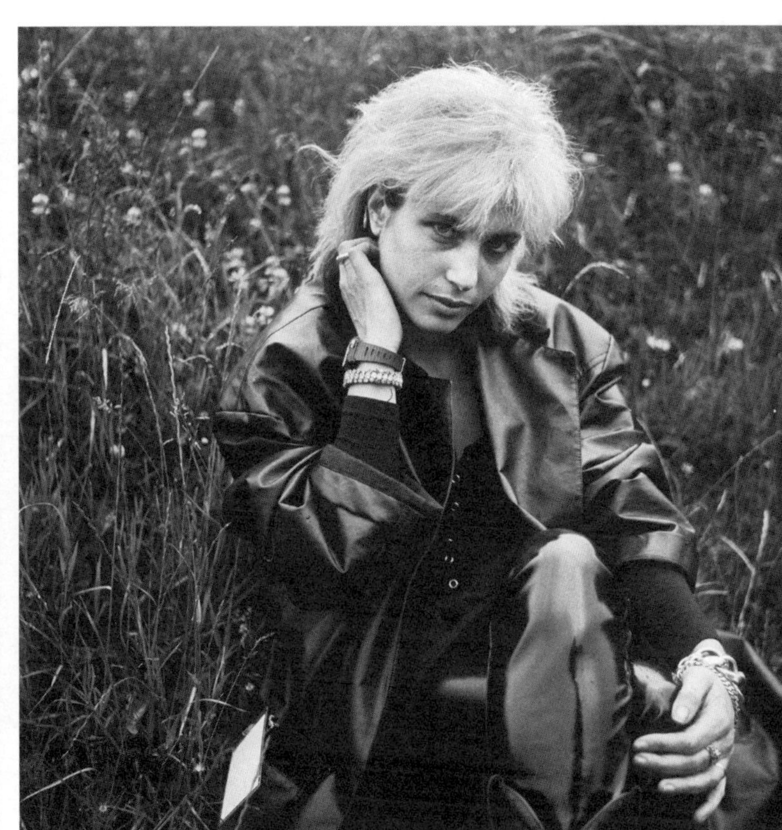

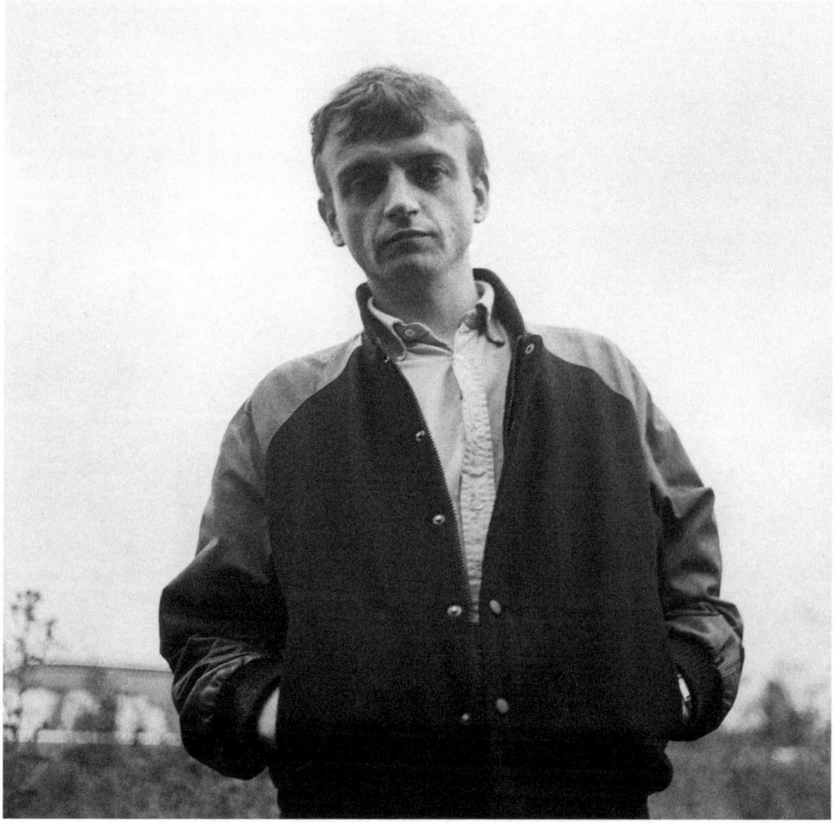

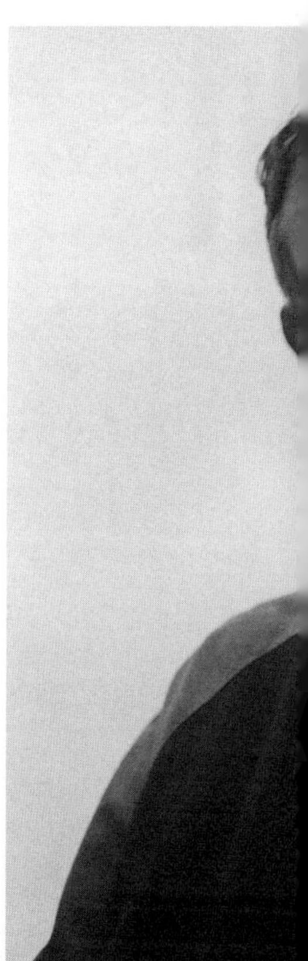

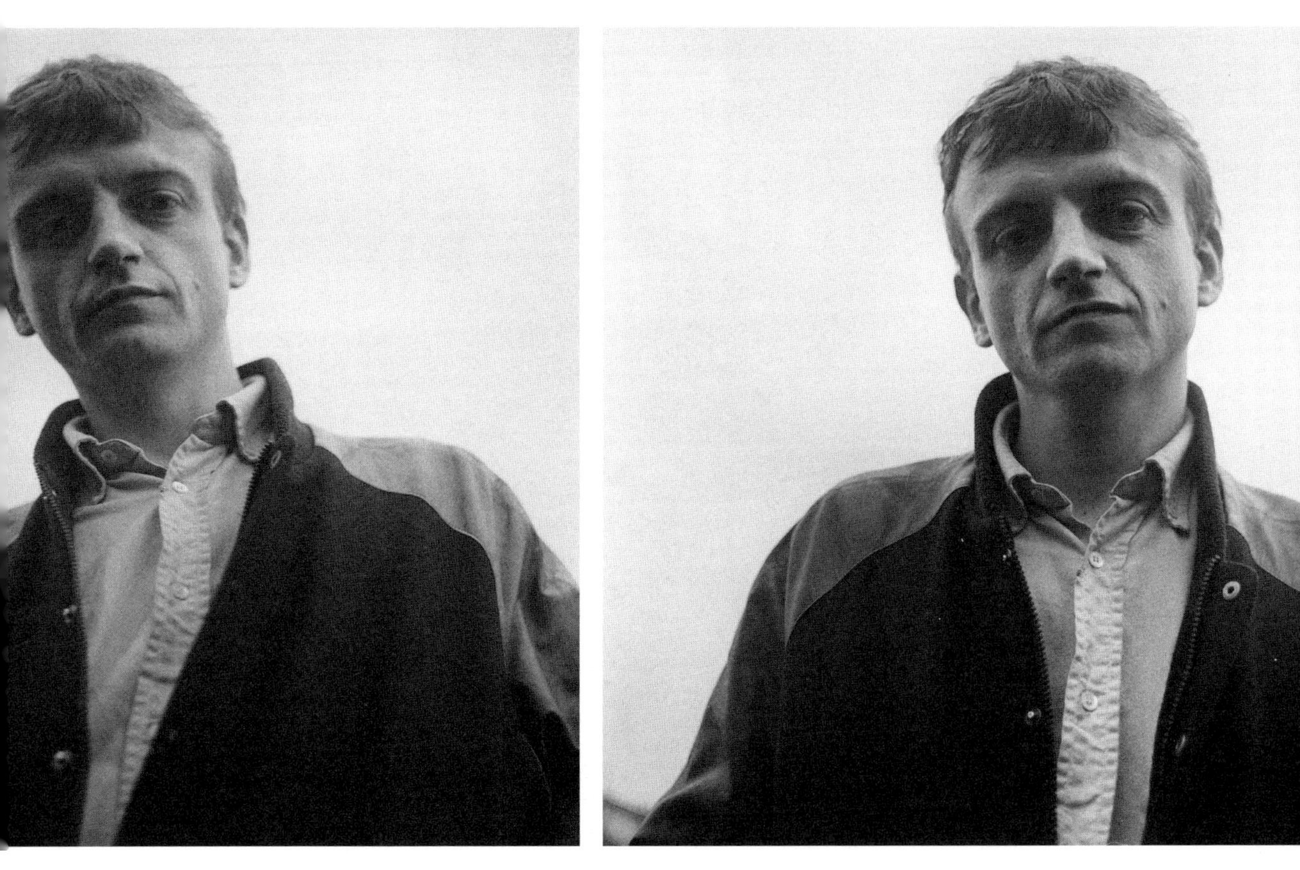

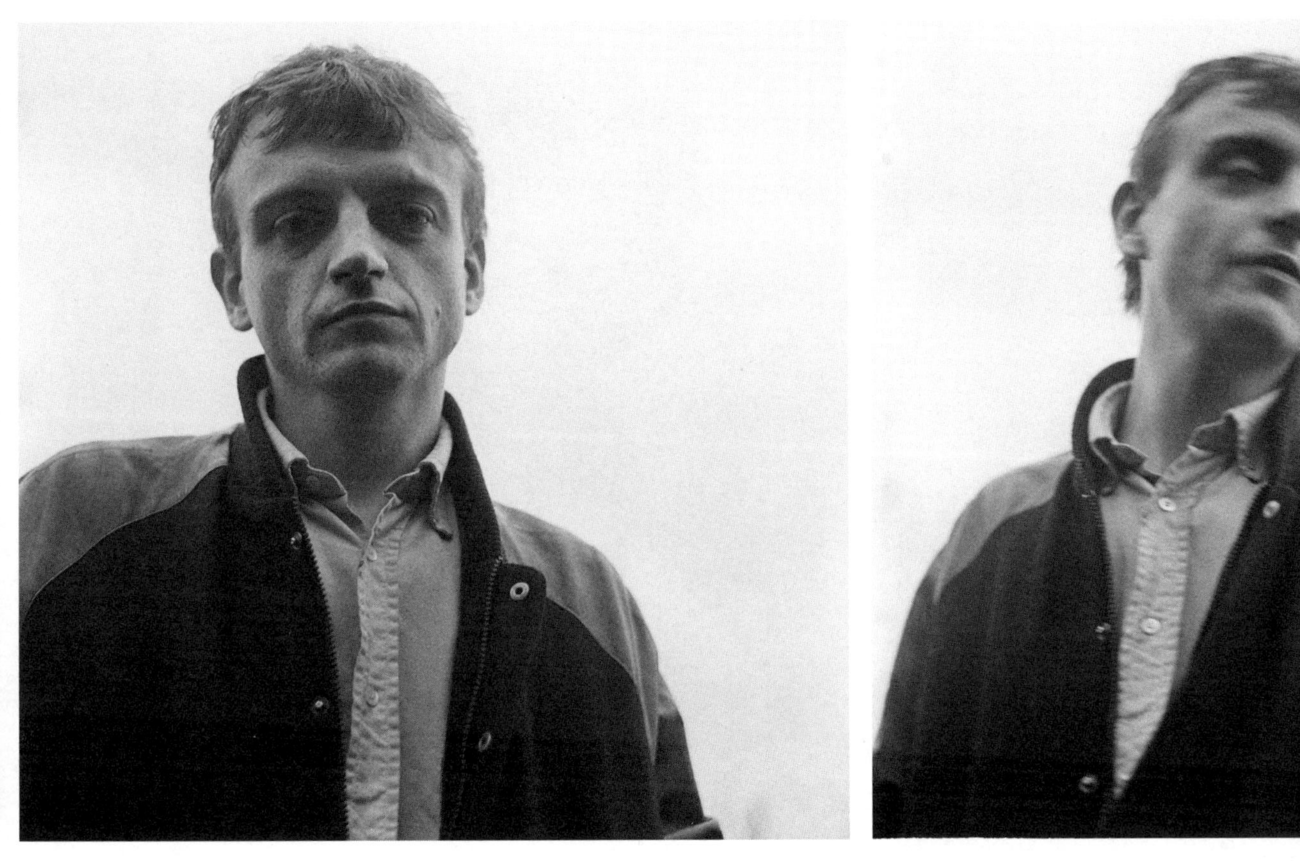

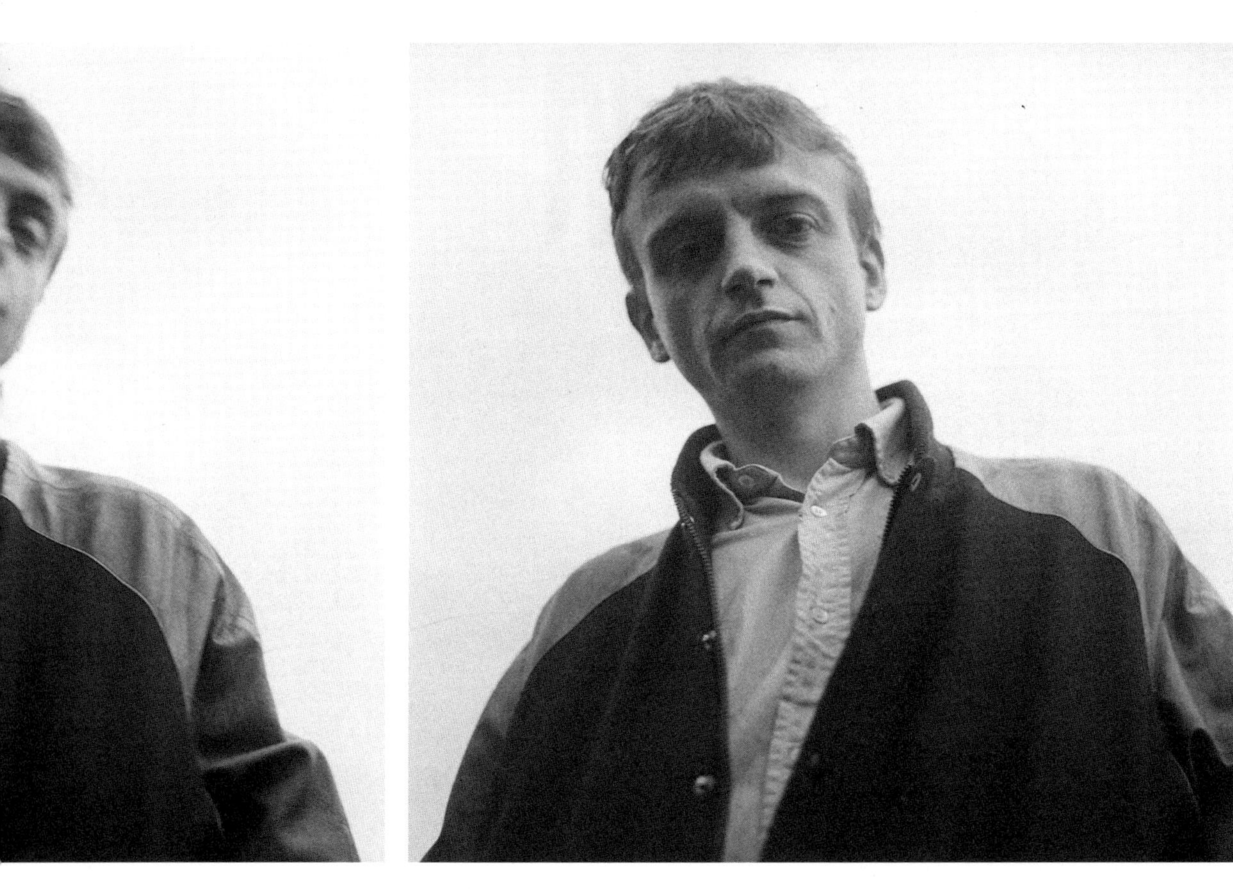